Reading Eliot's story is an ushering into the holy grace of God everywhere—the art of "now" that could make life a masterpiece.

Ann Voskamp, author of
One Thousand Gifts: A Dare to Live Fully Right Where You Are

A Story Unfinished reminds us all that God is ever present and near. My heart is broken but my soul is inspired by this story, and I'm better for reading it. This book will grip you and change you. Eliot's story reminds us to cherish each day and live life to the fullest.

Brad Lomenick, president of Catalyst and author of *The Catalyst Leader*

Matt Mooney will take you on a remarkable journey of words through these pages. Expect laughter, tears, and to fall in love with a boy named Eliot. With his conversational style and relatable insights, Matt is a guide who will get you to a place of new perspective where you're more fully alive in every way than when you first began.

Holley Gerth, best-selling author of *You're Already Amazing*

Within the pages of *A Story Unfinished*, Matt Mooney weaves together the surprising heights and heartbreaking depths of ninety-nine days with his son, Eliot. In so doing, he challenges us all to see the beauty that God has crafted within the painful realities that we all will face.

Mark Merrill, president of Family First and author of
All Pro Dad: Seven Essentials to Be a Hero to Your Kids.

With wit and honesty and a winsome way with words, Matt Mooney invites readers into the interior of loss—a place where life is cherished, sorrow becomes a companion, questions are allowed to simmer without easy answers, and beauty begins to blossom in the dark.

Nancy Guthrie, author of *Holding on to Hope* and
Hearing Jesus Speak into Your Sorrow

A STORY Unfinished

99 DAYS WITH ELIOT

MATT MOONEY

BEACON HILL PRESS

Copyright 2013
by Matthew Lyle Mooney and Beacon Hill Press of Kansas City

ISBN 978-0-8341-3011-1

Printed in the
United States of America

Cover Design: Ryan Deo
Internal Design: Sharon Page

10 9 8 7 6 5 4 3 2 1

CONTENTS

ACKNOWLEDGMENTS

To the rascals.
This is what I want you to know.

Thanks to

- My personal editor and encourager, Hillary Rector.
- Jon and Andrea as well as the cast and crew at Onyx Coffee Labs who allowed me to park and type for hours at a time.
- All who fed us, showed up at birthday parties, prayed for us and took care of us—so that we could take care of our son.
- Paul and Heather, Josh, Becky. No words suffice.
- Our parents and families who have walked with us, encouraged us and loved us so well.
- Ginny. You have shown me Christ through your life and your mothering. I love you.

INTRODUCTION

At thirty weeks pregnant my wife, Ginny, and I were informed that our child had a genetic disease. We were told that birth was unlikely, that life was not viable, and that a bleak future awaited.

We were *not* told that we would get ninety-nine days with our child. We were *not* told that those precious days would forever change us. We did *not* know the love and hurt that awaited.

No prerequisite is necessary to imagine the sharp pain—the inherent ache that comes with such a loss—it is precisely as one would guess: the sleepless nights, the unrelenting desire for answers, the frightening reality that slides in where optimism once resided.

Such is grief—zany and wild and unpredicted. But for us there is another unexpected facet, equaled in strength by the pain of the loss. This is the part of the story that we want others to hear, because it is the part of the story we could never have imagined. Thus, this is the treasure found on faraway shores we would rather have not explored.

Whereas pain came in the front door, an uninvited guest bellowing and kvetching like an obnoxious drunk, another came as well. Beauty came—from where I cannot say—as a stranger to sit with us in silence, although *beauty* is not an adequate description. Neither is *life* nor *peace* nor *clarity*, although they all came too.

It was God. He was near.

And at the very time I wanted to yell out asking where He was, I could not do so, because the air dripped with the reality of His presence, more evident than I have known before or since. The God who would not do what I asked of Him did not leave me, but instead, He came near.

Before

PART 1

One
FEAR OF FATHER

Eleven weeks pregnant. I made my way to the depressing second-level section of the law library. An Ozark winter had set in, and I forfeited battling the cold by wearing a thin zip-up sweater. I couldn't see the value in hauling around my warmer coat all day, to wear it only for the four-minute hike from my parking spot to the library door. Besides, denying my own desires was part of the gig. I reminded myself that I was going to be studying all day; warmth could take a backseat. With a slight chattering of teeth, I spread the books onto the table. I was determined to be focused.

For me, the first semester of law school had produced more time worrying about finals than actually doing anything school-related. The final grade in each class came down to one test at the end of the year. This struck me as a cruel way to structure things. I pictured myself letting my wife know that I had failed at law school and was fresh out of ideas for our future.

Of course, if I flunked out she wouldn't care. Without missing a beat, Ginny would assure me that the school had missed out on a great thing and that the teacher who failed me must have had a pathetic upbringing that yielded intimidation and insecurity upon being confronted with obvious signs of intelligence.

"Yep, they're gonna regret that one," she would say.

Were she the type to care about such things as law school success, she would have been long gone. The Lord knows I had given her ample ammunition in recent months to forego the good-wife role and tell me just to get a job. In six months she had smiled through two moves, and now I had dropped us squarely into her nightmare—Fayetteville, Arkansas.

Having grown up in a farming community of five thousand in the Louisiana delta, she had already made the decision to spend the rest of her years exploring a life not found in small towns. She bit her faithful lip, but we both knew she preferred cities—the bigger the better. She swears that cities reveal God's creativity.

Her adjustment to Fayetteville had been slow. There was a great farmer's market but no one to accompany her. Meanwhile, I had no strong feelings either way about our newfound community that was equal parts hippie holdover and college town. I had grown up in Arkansas, moved on, and had no plans of a return trip, but things had not been going to plan as of late.

Prior to Fayetteville, I had pulled Ginny out of a town we both loved, telling her that if we didn't move now, we would be in Fort Worth forever. As someone who fancies himself a free spirit, this seemed an obvious worst-case scenario. So in the way she does, she bought it; more *for* me than *from* me. While she slipped into a love affair with Nashville, I began to look for a job.

Before fleeing to Tennessee, my quarter-century of life had pretty-much been exactly the way I would have scripted it: easy and comfortable with an arm-candy kind of wife. God was good, because my life was good. The script was fine by me.

Until Nashville.

In Fort Worth I had taken my first real job out of college. I got paid to work with junior high and high school students. "Paid" may be somewhat of an overstatement for my position as the area director of a local ministry. Perks included free dental work from a sympathetic gentleman on the board of directors as well as the keys to a rat-infested house. I hate everything mouse related—even Disney World. More than once I have been spotted squealing atop a table and pointing to an area where I saw movement. Upon talk of marriage, I told Ginny that I would do all the "man" stuff—kill spiders, grill meats, research strange noises, and so on. But I would not deal with mice, rats, or the largest of the breed—possums. This was an integral part of the deal. And she obliged.

Thus, there could be only one reason that I was willing to stay in that mouse house—I loved the job. And although I was young, I knew that most of my peers did not share this affinity for their work. The Fort Worth kids would pull up in a Lexus to invite me to join them at some restaurant I knew I could not afford. They did not seem to notice that I had no money, so I never brought it up. I politely declined their invitation and instead invited them to help me set out traps.

The vast majority of my time with these confused beings still shy of independence consisted of video games, variations of any competition involving a basketball hoop, and rolls of duct tape, which was primarily used to strap each other to the wall. But when you gain the trust of persons in this age bracket, they slowly begin to bring their baggage with them and expect you to help them sort through it.

And right about here, I realized that I was sheltered.

For reasons unknown to me, the fact that I could smoke them on original Nintendo prompted these kids to bring their harsh realities to me: eating disorders, physical abuse, suicide. *Sheltered* sounds so negative, but my parents must have succeeded. As far as struggles in my own life went, I could think of only two. Both were related to sports, and both were quite a pathetic parallel when serving as one's resource for these realities.

I quit being the fourth-grade quarterback when Coach Mann yelled at me, opting for the defensive unit, where the coach was a bit mellower. Continuing the tragic tale, I sat on the bench my junior year on the basketball team with the burning knowledge that I was better than the starting point guard. Both of these injustices made me cry quite a bit more than I am revealing.

That's all I had. I could not relate to real pain. Not to these kids who were looking to me, not to the news I saw on television, not to anything that whispered of deep heartache. To me this seemed best. One thing I knew in observance of others' pain was that it warranted continued avoidance. I devised some sort of map that helped me navigate the pain of others, but admittedly, the map was cliché, and the main goal was to detour hard realities.

The church also kept me keenly aware of my lack of anything to grieve. Scripture does not allow a bypass of pain—heartache and loss are everywhere. The pains I so deftly avoided are actually sold as part of the package deal in the life of one who believes.

The Bible is full of deep valleys and pain that we tend to ignore upon retellings at backyard Bible schools: the first parents endured the murder of their son, David was depressed, Job was the poster boy for pain.

Jesus went so far as to ensure troubles and then made good on this guarantee with all those close to Him. But for me, anguish was a stranger. I remember sitting in the pew and listening along as the guy at the podium told the story behind the hymn "It Is Well with My Soul" as we all prepared to sing along in unison. The hymn was penned aboard a ship by a father as he crossed over the spot where his four daughters had died aboard a sinking vessel just days earlier.

> When peace like a river attendeth my way,
>   When sorrows like sea billows roll,
>   Whatever my lot, Thou hast taught me to say,
>   "It is well, it is well with my soul."

I sang it out—each word of all the verses. Despite Coach Mann's shrill screams and my time spent filling water bottles that junior season, my voice rose with all the conviction I could muster.

Yes, it was well with my soul.

Until Nashville.

Apparently, there are a lot of young people in Nashville, and all of them had something to offer employers that I did not. I could not get a job.

I began by looking for jobs that I actually thought I wanted, and I continued until I was declined by every bookstore and coffee shop in a twenty-mile radius. Ginny had been supporting us with her merchandising job at a clothing retailer. With Christmas approaching and after four months of making myself do nothing but job-search daily from 8 A.M. to 5 P.M., Ginny was able to swing me a job (as a favor to her)—I folded sweaters at The Gap.

I quickly ascended the ranks and became loved by the managers for two qualities: sobriety and punctuality. I loathed the job. Every day was life's little Post-it note that I was a failure. It wasn't the fact that it was retail—I had done that multiple times before. But the Nashville move had been made in hopes of adventure and memories, a risky leap that was sure to turn out in storybook manner. The two of us had always talked of our disdain for *picket fences*. This was our code signaling the typical script of a typical couple—the ones who smile a lot and have great lawns.

But steering clear of the Joneses was not getting us any closer to what we wanted. I folded sweaters by the dozens and sweatshirts by the hundreds, all the while devising witty answers for those who asked what I did and why we had moved to Nashville if we were not aspiring musicians.

I let the dream die one particular day in the mall. Wiping down the plastic table, we took our seats. Ginny unpacked turkey sandwiches as we discussed if we could afford to split a fountain drink. We agreed to save the money for a date night. Ducking my head in an attempt to hide the obvious, I pretended the tears were not happening and stumbled through an attempt to explain how sorry I was that I had moved her here—away from friends and the place she loved—to work in the mall together. I tried to feign confidence that it was just a season, fumbling through a pep talk on how I would come up with something. She let me finish before making it clear that she already thought we were fine and she certainly wasn't waiting on my grand scheme to save the day. Not long after this lunch, and somewhere around folding hooded sweatshirt number three thousand twelve, I thought law school sounded good.

If Nashville served as the introduction to a life that did not go swimmingly, it also revealed a propensity to rely on myself by devising alternate routes around painful potholes instead of traveling through them. So I headed back to school to get a law degree, all the while fairly certain that I didn't want to be a lawyer. And Ginny just smiled and helped me load the Arkansas-bound U-Haul to head away from a city she loved and toward a place she would rather not go.

Therefore, flunking out of law school was not an option. I would pass these upcoming finals, and Ginny would like me. Delving into a too-thick book that day in the library, I reminded myself of all that was riding on my ability to answer these questions at the proper time: my life.

Our recent affinity for home-hopping now seemed but a small drop in a large ocean of insecurity. Predictably, my mind quickly wandered from copious notes on civil procedure. There are seasons of life when monumental life changes come in droves.

Ginny was pregnant.

It had not been easy to accept this reality. I remember checking the home pregnancy thing seven times. We had opted for the cheaper, three-pack version, the one that merely gave an addition sign for a positive pregnancy test. It never dawned on me that the meager addition-sign version might be insufficient until I spotted the five-dollar upgraded, top-of-the-line model, which apparently bought a full-blown "You're Pregnant" for one's reading pleasure.

In the store I had scoffed at the lavish morons who would fork over an additional five dollars for a readable stick. But now, staring at these undeniable intersecting lines, I felt as though the more expensive one must be better. Yes, I would feel more certain about this whole idea of a person growing inside my wife if I had the newest, most advanced, readable stick on the market. How could one base life's biggest piece of breaking news on an inferior product? Besides, I didn't trust her aim. She was a novice. With years of accuracy practice under my belt, even I would have struggled to direct the spray precisely.

Ginny was giddy with laughter. Poor her, I thought. She was buying it. Apparently she had not realized that I had picked the generic stick.

"Ninety-nine point nine percent," she said as she kept pointing and reading from the box label.

"Exactly" I replied, as if she had proven my point for me.

Any idea this preposterously big takes time to swallow.

L-I-F-E . . .

B-A-B-Y . . .

F-A-T-H-E-R . . .

Even though we had been wanting and waiting—daresay, expecting—it's just the type of moment I unwittingly imagined must always be accompanied by big background music like Beethoven or Mariah Carey. But no musical accompaniment, just Ginny's laugh followed by my imploring her to "Do it again. We've got two more."

I don't remember the moment I crossed the line of accepting that I was actually going to be a father. It seems more of a process than a line anyway. A few days pass before realizing that the baby is not coming tomorrow. Days are a good thing when you're trying to change every single thing you hate about yourself.

The demarcation of parenthood provides an opportunity for the equivalent of a colossal New Year's resolution list: I'll be kinder to people when I have the baby; I won't cuss when the little tyke is here; we will all exercise together as a family.

And for me this was about the time subtle fears began creeping in. Color me naive, but I do not think I had known fear in an intimate way prior to the news of a baby. But trepidation was tethered to fatherhood for me—and rode in sidesaddle as a part of the deal.

Some of it was just that I wasn't where or who I wanted to be when I became a father. But the larger part was feeling as if I were opening up my heart. It was an unfamiliar movement of which I had faint knowledge. Though marriage had hinted of a love containing peaks and depths beyond anywhere I had gone, this was different.

I had chosen my spouse—and in doing so, only after much deliberation, I had willingly allowed someone into a sacred space behind the curtain, one I had stitched together through the years, having learned the value of a divider. It served more as a shield than a curtain, but this little one was coming with no deliberation allowed.

Children introduce their parents to an unprecedented vulnerability even before birth. They dive headfirst into your heart— to the places where the deepest love is stored. Fear accompanies their arrival, stemming from a subconscious awareness that the space where they land is the holding tank for great pain as well.

An unknown person was receiving an all-access pass to places of me that, until now, I did not even know existed. As opposed to the calculated nature of marriage, this child was happening *to* me. How could I have such thoughts and fears for someone I had never met?

I do not know when I relented to the fact that I was actually a father. But it occurred somewhere around my acceptance that someone was coming who could break my heart, and instead of avoidance, I ran headlong.

Yes, I was going to be a father.

I was shocked. Sure, I realized the physical mechanics of how this all worked. But I was going to be a dad. Grappling with this realization brought alternating waves of hope and fear.

It seemed to me that creating and raising a real, live person would have all the makings of adventure and lifetime memories that I so desperately craved. However, law school doesn't pay well. While most of my friends had settled into lives whereby kids seemed to fit, I was months removed from referring to myself as a "Gap girl," headed back to school for a degree I didn't intend to use, and I still enjoyed a good bowl of Lucky Charms.

So I spent my first semester sorting through questions of jurisdiction along with ones of whether or not I would be the one to cut the umbilical cord. There was no way I was cutting that cord. Of all the questions circling my head, this seemed the easiest one to answer. My goal would be not to pass out, with a backup goal of no one actually knowing I passed out if I happened to fail goal number one.

I'm not sure how many times I've passed out—a sure indicator that it's been too many. Always the same routine: I reassure those around me that I am fine; then I begin to slur and sway until finally dropping like a building imploding to make way for the new strip mall.

Although I had never been witness to the actual birthing process, I had talked to father friends who had. Their reports did not seem promising—a perfect concoction that leaves me tasting the floor. I was left wondering how this whole cord phenomenon ever came about. I couldn't devise one plausible scenario whereby cutting this mother rope had become en vogue and even created an expectation placed on an entire gender.

And it felt good to nail down the answer to at least one question. Fatherhood, law school, and life seemed evasive, but I knew this—I wasn't about to cut that cord.

Two
SWIRL

If I let fear drive, I'll miss all the places love wants to take me.
—Dawn Carter

I remember the first compact disc I ever purchased. The whole idea of a laser disc was newfangled technology. Exhibiting signs in pre-pubescence of the tightwad to come, I questioned what exactly was worth the extra two dollars that I could not get from a cassette. In yet another sign of things to come, I fell victim to the lure of progress and coughed up what comprised the entirety of my holdings and investments for the compact disc.

After wrestling with the plastic antitheft packaging for thirteen minutes, a process that left me already hoping for the next type of music delivery—one that would not require a quarter hour of my life to break into what I had purchased—I gently placed the shiny disc into the boom box I had recently received for Christmas.

Throbbing sounds in pitches heretofore unknown reverberated through my room and off my red metal bunk bed. I was fully convinced that I had arrived as a man. Well, in the name of full disclosure, there was a little hiccup that made this memory not quite as seamless as conveyed. On the first pass at my manhood, I had pushed the giant triangle for "Play"—but nothing occurred. A quick reference to the user's manual prompted me to turn the CD over, words up, and only then did the notes stream through the room, my testosterone rising and falling with the volume levels.

I listened for hours to Rob Base accompanied by what was at this time a mandatory sidekick—DJ Easy Rock. I wish I could say that this particular CD could be attributed to a short period of my life, but I clearly recall the lyrics of "It Takes Two" ringing out the rolled-down windows of my Mustang, the one I drove in college.

In these early days of compact disc magic I would listen for hours. For reasons still unknown, I had a childhood fascination with learning the words of the songs—every word of every song—so much so that in days before Google was a verb, I sat and wrote down each lyric: pushing "Pause," backing up, pushing "Play," then "Pause" again, necessary steps in order to jot down the intelligible syllables. I continued, repeating this series of pathetic events while perched in front of my Sony like a factory worker, never expanding my output over a seven-word increment and pushing my lousy short-term memory to the brink.

Though I knew them all by heart, there were two songs off this album that normal people around my age might have actually heard on the radio. I already alluded to "It Takes Two," the one that served as the title for the entire record and is still actually getting some airtime—although rarely now and only as a tip of the hat to those of us not yet comfortable with being shown respect for our age. Other than "It Takes Two," the other chart-topper from the CD that still holds captive more gray matter of my brain than I care to admit was "Joy and Pain." If the tan velour sweat-suit worn on the cover does not sufficiently signal that this was a different day, how about the fact that I could print all the lyrics without "#*%*#" to hide the naughty words? I will not print out all of the words, tempting as it is to clearly demonstrate the great-ness exuding from this track, because there are over four hundred seventy-five words. (I just googled it.) But I will type out the cho-rus in its entirety for you and ask you at some point to open your mind to the possibility that genius is overlooked on a daily basis and implore you to examine this rap ballad for yourself: *Joy and pain, like sunshine and rain.*

I have to say that I think Base and Rock have managed to capture the quintessential life theology of most humans in seven words. Though Rob Base makes an unregrettable first purchase in my move to compact discs, a life lived under the banner of these seven words is regrettable indeed. I don't know if hours hunched over my jambox jotting notes is what did it for me—or if I can blame Rob at all. If I had half the charisma—or chest hair for that matter—of Rob Base, I would have spit out these lyrics myself. I believed every word of this nursery rhyme. And though I would like to blame the sneaky influence of rap music and paint red devil horns on my youth's hero (ones that match the shade of his un-zipped wind suit) I cannot. Truth is, I did not need Rob to build a world whereby pain and joy were mutually exclusive events—as stark in their opposition to one another as sun and rain. I crafted that world myself and sought only the sun.

These days we have a saying oft repeated in the Mooney house, and it will not sell any records, although I will be happy to don a velour sweat-suit if requested.

We play in the rain.

When clouds form on the horizon, when claps of thunder stiffen the hairs on your neck, when all those around you are running inside to the safety of their homes and telling you to do the same—go outside.

I have best seen the sun as it shimmers through drops of rain, as it cracks through the clouds with breathtaking radiance—the very ones I wanted to run from.

My son changed my tune. It is sunshine *with* rain. I would much prefer to learn through theory the monolithic lessons learned only through walking the road. The corpulent one wiping the casserole drippings from his mouth may have read the book on hunger, but no matter the notes he has taken, his mouth will not salivate at the thought of lunch.

It was Eliot who introduced me to the pangs of true hunger. Before him, I had not known dark nights of the soul, having only read books or heard murmurs of a beauty born from ashes. Before Eliot, I had nodded and amen-ed those things that I could not actually grasp in a life lived pursuing sun with a fervor matched only by the intensity by which I avoided the rain.

Eliot's life points squarely to Christ and has colored my own life in more ways than these pages can hope to contain. In fact, some of the most meaningful gleanings will remain unearthed as I still have yet to find sufficient words to convey them. The following is my attempt to lasso the wind, corralling my thoughts into patterns of how his life changed my own. May your own bellies grow loud as you examine a life that I cannot do justice to but am honored beyond words to behold.

CARNIES

As is the case with most of life's monumental shifts, I cannot recall a precise moment in time when my son completely obliterated all the tenets I spent a lifetime crafting. But he did—or God did through Him. These shifts began even before we knew he was a boy or that his name would be Eliot, and long before ever hearing the word *trisomy*.

I held a lot of cups as a kid. In my town, the annual coming of the fair was a rite of passage for the area's teens and tweens. We traveled in coed packs—amoebas of awkwardness weaving and bobbing through the rope ladders, trailers with tiny people, and endless invitations from nomadic strangers to spend our yellow tickets at their booth. Beyond this maze of gaming existed three additional fair neighborhoods: there was the suburb of food—lemonades, kettle corn, and a smattering of items edible only when battered. Next, the ribbon-wearing animals were relegated to row upon row of covered metal buildings from which emanated smells that left me unable to enjoy my funnel cake. Last came the main reason that those I traveled with had come at all: the rides. I did not share the affinity of my cohorts; I hated the rides. So I held cups, stuffed animals, and purses as the rest of the pack lined up for the Swinging Dragon.

As is custom in these childhood days, the ones I have since worked hard to suppress, every single person at the fair within earshot attempted some form of coercion in order to get me, the homely-looking kid with oversized glasses, to go and experience the time of my life. But I would have none of it. The more they bargained, the farther I dug my heels into what I hoped was mud.

Even before the fair, I avoided the things that I was scared of and endured the cost associated with so doing. No one had to teach me to navigate around those things that I believed were to my detriment. I did so fiercely, even with the added weight of peer pressure pushing me elsewhere. I intrinsically sought my own happiness, never questioning that I knew precisely where it could be found. Fair rides were for me merely emblematic of a larger life doctrine: those things I disliked were to be avoided and placed into a bucket named *Bad*, whereas the things that make me happy—the *Good*—were to be sought and piled one atop another in an altogether separate and far better bucket. This formula for life, born in my subconscious and never actually acknowledged, measured joy by counting the items in the bucket labeled *Good* and offsetting their measure with a discount accounting for all the bucket of *Bad*.

The world only served to feed and coddle this hypothesis— the one that I could only begin to actually see once it had been blown to bits and lay around me in pieces like a puzzle. With his piercing almond eyes, Eliot would bring the tension of paradox into my life of seeking comfort. For with him came the greatest measure of beauty I have known. It came masked in something most certainly bound for the bucket of items to avoid. I did not cede my life's theory willingly. In Eliot I was forced to abandon it. Because of him, I plunged headfirst into raging waters. Because of him, I put down the cup, handed over my ticket, and stepped in line. Because of him, I found joy in the least likely of places.

BOTH AND . . .

Tucked away in Genesis lies a strange tale of Jacob and his wrestling with a man. Although Jacob plainly asks for his wrestling opponent's name, the stranger does not comply. In spite of the silence, Jacob walks away pinpointing the foe as God himself. Jacob wrestled with God.

> And Jacob was left alone. And a man wrestled with him until the breaking of the day. When the man saw that he did not prevail against Jacob, he touched his hip socket, and Ja-

cob's hip was put out of joint as he wrestled with him. Then he said, "Let me go, for the day has broken." But Jacob said, "I will not let you go unless you bless me." And he said to him, "What is your name?" And he said, "Jacob." Then he said, "Your name shall no longer be called Jacob, but Israel, for you have striven with God and with men, and have prevailed." Then Jacob asked him, "Please tell me your name." But he said, "Why is it that you ask my name?" And there he blessed him. So Jacob called the name of the place Peniel, saying, "For I have seen God face to face, and yet my life has been delivered." The sun rose upon him as he passed Peniel, limping because of his hip (*Genesis 32:24-31*, ESV).

It would seem as if this bout with God actually goes a few rounds as Jacob will not relent until he receives the blessing that he seeks. Now I think that if this *man* would have been so inclined, he could have pulled out his God card and given it a swipe, leaving Jacob eating his meals through a straw. But Jacob wrestled, and he was commended for it with a blessing of colossal importance. His name was changed to "Israel"—a reminder of the impact that God was going to undertake through him.

Thus, Jacob runs with reckless abandon down a path that must certainly end with his demise. He leans into his fears and clings tightly, asking for blessing, begging for good to come from an encounter that seems anything but good for those sitting in the cheap seats. And the God who could plunder his life instead rewards him greatly. God wanted to wrestle. God wanted to give.

But Jacob did not receive only the blessing. Intertwined with great promise comes a wound. He walked away with a limp. His blessing came at a price. There was no way Jacob could receive the blessing and not receive the limp, though I am certain he would have chosen as much if this option were on the table. It was not.

The limp came with the blessing. Forever his wounded gait would point to the time he gazed upon the face of God.

Through my six-pound son, I found that joy and pain are not mutually exclusive buckets. Unfortunately, life does not allow for such a system. Containers may let us compartmentalize our physical world into an organized reality that seems tidy, but a life spent striving to cram day-to-day occurrences into labeled spaces is a sad pursuit. Eliot's life and leaving helped me see life's events more in terms of finger-paintings than paint buckets.

While pails are labeled spaces reserved for monochromatic ingredients, finger paints are a sloppy smattering where they all bleed together. These plastic containers of paint—green trays with hollowed out circles reserved for primary hues—have managed to evade society's propensity for reinvention; not one detail seems to have changed since I was the one holding the brush and being told to paint on the paper and not on the table. This simple mainstay of childhood has replaced *buckets* as my go-to metaphor for understanding all that comes our way, for the beauty and the mess enter only when the paint escapes the space that was created to contain it.

These days the double doors of our refrigerator—or for that matter, any blank space on the wall—serve dutifully as a revolving museum dedicated to the day's creation. The tabletop, acting as a studio, is often unseen due to a smattering of crayons, markers, or paints. The paints must always be monitored with the watchful eye of a prom chaperone; it does not take long for our entire house to morph into some sort of motif in which Rainbow Bright apparently lost her lunch.

Under watchful eye, the colors are taken out and applied to a canvas. Only when they interact with one another and swirl together can true beauty be created. Life and its reality are always a bit messier than any manmade bucket attempting to delineate the good from the bad, the beauty from the pain. If all events pass through the hand of God, and we are told they do, then it seems that He is really bad at placing items in the buckets we have outlined for Him. Instead, He swirls it all together until we are unable to separate and label where the good began and the bad ended.

We do not get to pick the ways in which God chooses to reveal himself. Please understand what I am *not* saying. The loss of Eliot is bad, big-bucket *Bad,* and I make no attempt to tie a bow on our own experience nor the immense pain I come across in the lives of others. I miss him every day. However, in being forced onto a ride I would have evaded at all costs, I found treasures beyond measure that came trouncing into my tidy life along with the pain. When screams of fear tell us to sit the ride out, may we instead ask for faith to accept that our sought path of avoiding pain at all costs may also avoid God.

"My thoughts are not your thoughts, neither are your ways my ways," declares the LORD. "As the heavens are higher than the earth, so are my ways higher than your ways and my thoughts than your thoughts" (*Isaiah 55:8-9*).

If His ways are not my ways, then I must be willing to go places I have not chosen, stepping forward with a resolute faith, willing to die to the map my mind has crafted, and hope in Him. Priorities of His kingdom run counter to priorities of the world— every time in every way.

The way to what we want is seldom obtained by grasping for it in the manner that seems most rational to us. Endless media outlets provide daily reminders that many who simply seek happiness find anything but what they set out to find. When we follow our noses, trusting the fragrances that smell to us of life, we instead often arrive at death. Sometimes it is the kind of death that makes headlines, but more often it is the slow death of realizing one's life has been wasted. We cannot trust our senses when it is true life that we seek. As humans, we seem sadly programmed to reach for appearance rather than substance, and when we take hold of that which we pursued, we find that it is but a mirage—one in opposition to what we wanted in the first place. Scripture points repeatedly to this counterintuitive nature of pursuing greater things.

To be first, we should be last. The greatest one will be the servant. To live, we must die.

Jesus in His first recorded sermon serves only to turn our world even more inside-out with an outline of priorities He seeks to usher in with His kingdom. Pushing aside the tidy buckets outlined by the religious types—where strict adherence results in your bucket of *Good* being filled to the brim and a lack of doing results in your *Bad* bucket being filled—He dips into the green plastic tray of paints and depicts a kingdom with values so swirled and upside down that we—the inhabitants of this world—can only be baffled, dazed but drawn to the canvas by a tale of another land, one in which we actually grasp that which our heart desires and our hands reach toward.

Blessed are the poor in spirit, for theirs is the kingdom of heaven (*Matthew 5:3*).
I want the blessing. I want to take possession of the Kingdom. I do not want to be poor in spirit.

Blessed are those who mourn, for they will be comforted (*Matthew 5:4*).
I want to be blessed. I want to be comforted. I do not want to mourn.

I want my name changed, but I do not want to limp. I want buckets—ones with labels. I want to know all that God showed me of himself through my son—for I now know of things I merely spoke of before holding Eliot.

But I want Eliot still here with me.

I do not want the daily pain of missing him. I do not want to consult photographs to remember the contours of his face.

But when God comes near, the glory and majesty of His being pierce the brokenness of us and our world. Even the dark is light in Him.

He often comes in the last place we were looking.

The reality of this shift—from buckets of *Good* and *Bad* to finger paintings depicting a life accounting for both—finds me attempting to live life against the grain of my own desires. Since Eliot, I have a harder time making decisions, as I trust my own inclinations less. I weigh and measure and pray a little longer, fearful that I would willingly avoid the wrestling but also forfeit the blessing.

In Eliot I leaned into my greatest fear and found joy and pain intimately linked together. If we avoid the route fraught with pain at all costs, then we may end up avoiding the blessing that God has for us as well. I could not receive Eliot and not also receive the greatest ache I have ever known. Although I would take away the pain, I would never take away that with which the pain came, and in this way I would take it all again. The things I pursued came in with the very things I spent my life avoiding. In this life I limp. But if I hobble by and you stop to listen, I will tell of my encounter with God and the blessing I received.

Three
PREPARATION

Twelve to twenty weeks pregnant. Ginny was eating and gagging and growing. She had never been the salad-as-meal type, and her penchant for ample portions had apparently been placed on steroids by conception. I know most women will dismiss this as sentiment, but Ginny's healthy appetite held huge attraction for me early on in our dating. She ordered steak and dessert before baby— and now an appetizer too.

As for the heaves, she rarely actually vomited during pregnancy; rather, she was left wishing she could—awkward gags accompanying each breath. Pregnancy is an awkward junior high dance all over again. I think this is true for both parties, but most assuredly from the male perspective. The birthing process is most commonly described with words like "beautiful" or "radiant," but this is a worldwide snow job of epic proportions, a conspiracy surely founded on intentions of continuing the human race. Help me see the beauty inherent in the standard birth-class tutorial video. If camcorder-quality footage with seventies-vintage wide-angle shots of some blonde woman giving birth naturally is supposed to be a learning tool, mission accomplished. I'm happy to be male, and that's got to hurt.

I was not adequately equipped for the stark realities associated with pregnancy. And they just kept coming. It seemed to me that something, possibly a government-issued guidebook to fatherhood, should have tipped me off as to what was ahead. But nothing did. I guess it really never works that way. There are certain clubs throughout life whose membership requires an experience that cannot be foregone with payment of an admission fee. No manual will suffice for this one. You just have to walk through it.

Ginny and I decided we would hold out as long as possible before letting others in on our mammoth bun-in-the-oven revelation. This window of time when we were the only ones in the know was, in a strange way, quite fun and bonding. Numerous conversations included unspoken codes and winks whereby we acknowledged that these folks had no idea our lives were not actually as they perceived. We surmised that this must be what it feels like to be a genius; we were the smartest people in the room—no one knew what we knew. So we milked the power trip for all it was worth, devising strategies that allowed us to make sure we gave folks the exact same answers and replies that we would have when we were not with child.

Notwithstanding the Einstein feelings, we were dying to tell someone. So just shy of three months pregnant, we begin orchestrating family dinners and making some phone calls. While everyone played their roles admirably—the excess time had produced enormous buildup—the recipients were bound to let us down with any reaction that did not involve fireworks and juggling monkeys. Though the news is big to all of those surrounding you, the enormity is relative to your role.

We were beginning to meet some new folks in Fayetteville and had even managed to move past the awkward startup stage with a few of them. Ginny was hosting "chick nights." A couple of gals would come over to eat chicken and watch the latest installment of some silly show that I would typically look down on—but not now. I knew this was a good development, even if it was not good television. The coupling of pregnancy and possible friends had Ginny talking less of her top five cities to which we could move when I was finished with school.

She was acclimating—or at least distracted. Her days were comprised of incessant research, list-making, and gleaning information from other women who had managed to make another life. Although this mother dance has since been defined for me as "nesting," at the time I could refer to her only as "in need of valium." But, of course, that would not be good for the baby.

The amount of decisions accompanying a modern-day hatch can be quite overwhelming. It left me pining with sentimentality for the days of my own parents. They had two stroller options— buy it or don't. There are now two hundred models, each boasting of how they will make your child safer and more beautiful.

So we found ourselves arguing over things we knew nothing about. The same conversations echoed throughout the infant aisles of box stores every day:

"Honey, do we want the nipple that will leave the teeth intact or the slow-draining nipple that doesn't cause choking?"

Unfortunately for Ginny, I am the rare father-to-be who actually demands involvement in these tedious determinations most often left solely to women. For some reason, I insist on being included, and although most women sob and insist that this is what they want from their lousy spouse, I can assure you that it is not the case. There is little noble about a fifteen-minute forced discussion on which particular breast pump best mimics a suckle.

As we approached twenty weeks pregnant, and with surprisingly little discussion, it was agreed we would not find out the gender of the baby until he or she was born. Ginny brought it up, and I concurred; the mystery sounded fun. The decision in no way seemed monumental, but apparently we had made a miscalculation. None of the handbooks we perused had reported on the weight that this decision carried. Unbeknownst to us, we had squarely chosen a side in a debate we did not even know existed.

"You're not finding out?" a friend would say with disdain as we excitedly relayed our news of a forthcoming baby.

"Oh, you're *those* people," she would continue.

"What people?" we asked.

"Well, I could never . . ." was always the reply.

So began the seemingly never-ending conversation that wound through an interrogation on just how we were going to do the room or buy the clothes. How did we sleep? And was everything going to be yellow?

Due to naiveté, we were unprepared to answer the barrage, but over time we developed a script and stuck to it.

"Yes, we're *those* people."

"We're not really pink-and-blue folks anyway."

"No, we're not going to change our minds."

"Actually, we hate yellow, but we've heard there are other colors out there."

So having told our friends of the upcoming arrival, with gender script intact and a breast pump sufficiently emulating breastfeeding, we were ready to actually see this person—just not the gender-specifics.

DOCTORS

Twenty weeks and five days pregnant. Ginny pushed the "up" arrow on the elevator panel. The ride was unusually quiet. It was only a one-story trip, but it seemed like the Sears Tower. The day had come; and even though we were not finding out the sex, we still could not wait to lay eyes on what was going on beneath the now-evident bump in Ginny's jeans.

Of course, this meant Ginny had to sacrificially let me accompany her to the clinic.

I ask lots of questions. Being raised by a teacher, I like to think of this as a hunger for knowledge; however, a hunger for elementary explanation may be more accurate. I distrust any and all things that cannot be explained in a way that I truly understand—because if I cannot understand it, it must not make sense.

So with pregnancy I had questions.

I do not recall the point when I began to distrust an entire community. But this is the way I felt toward the population that refers to itself as "healthcare providers." It seems that such a disdain would be birthed from fantastic stories of how my grandfather's heart surgery was botched and he had paid with his life. And after weathering such storms, I could no longer be expected to place trust in any of them. But I had no such story—no reason to feel this way; I just did.

Of course, I was going to be at every appointment. This was a safeguard for our marriage. Otherwise, upon arrival home from the doctor, I would pepper Ginny with questions no human could possibly know the answers to.

So I started going to the gynecologist.

Pregnancy is such a cyclical season of life. The calendar used by everyone else is no longer sufficient. Your world is narrowed as all of life's happenings are now measured in light of the due date.

Therefore, amidst stirrups and color-coded charts of feminine areas I never knew existed, I probed our doctor on just how baby's arrival date would be derived. I fully expected her reply to incorporate at least one of the scary flipcharts or maybe break out a formula that incorporated *pi*.

Turns out that the equation giving rise to this life-changing date is seemingly archaic and simple. Yet this date sets the pattern of orbit for the foreseeable future. Vacation plans, decorating deadlines, and commitments of all kinds are all now funneled through a best-guess day of arrival.

"Ginny Mooney," the nurse bellowed, seemingly bored with our life-changing moment. We were drunk with anticipation. I jumped up, lockstep with my wife, to go see the little Mooney. But in true inebriated manner, I was left feeling sheepish upon notification that the first call was merely standard procedure. I wasn't needed for the prerequisite weigh-in and blood pressure cuff. It would be another fifteen minutes until the show. I feigned exasperation, but we both knew we were about to bear witness to something we had waited for our whole lives—to behold our child. I could wait fifteen minutes more.

It happened so fast. Ushered into an underwhelming, softly-lit room, we met the gal who was just doing her day job, and then, there on the screen, before we were ready, was our child. Although at first it requires assistance to even know what end is up, mysterious shapes join together in kaleidoscope fashion until the beginnings of a small person come into view. There on the screen—our child.

We laughed and pointed and gasped. On our way out we were handed small black-and-white pictures, along with a DVD—token mementos for later validation that it was not all a dream.

We strolled through the lobby on clouds into the elevator filled with chatter, zipping downward where we stopped to view the newborns through large windows.

The ultrasound had ushered in a new reality. There is something about being able to witness, to see what has as yet been invisible. What had been etched into the head was now seared into the heart. A baby was coming.

FRIENDS

Twenty-one weeks pregnant. Almost lost in the fireworks of the ultrasound was the news that there were some "things" that needed "watching." Of course, this sounded scary to each of us, but upon further explanation our hearts were back to a normal rhythm. We sat quiet, focused on each syllable, as we were told that there were some cysts on the brain, which were not all that unusual and often associated with development and typically disappear over time— but worth monitoring. Also, the umbilical cord was two-vessel instead of the expected three. Both of these announcements were delivered in a monotone manner by our doctor and followed by multiple questions of worst-case scenarios on my part.

As Dr. Partridge patiently answered each interrogatory that I offered up, I turned to set my eyes on Ginny. She turned to me as well, each of us looking for context—signs in the other as to whether this was a moment of huge proportion or one we would soon forget. There was no way of knowing, but we hunted every inch of the stale room, foraging for clues that might tell us how to feel, hanging on each of the doctor's words as if it might be her last, sizing up body language, inflection, and tone.

I felt that she truly wasn't worried, and I was a little surprised by a twinge of thankfulness toward this woman in whom I expected to find a foe. With her patience and directness, Dr. Partridge was winning me over. Her recommendation was for additional ultrasounds at twenty-five and thirty weeks along—merely as precaution. There was no need to worry, we were assured, and, besides, more opportunities for baby viewings didn't sound so bad.

We left with no lumps in our throats, keenly aware of experiencing feelings unknown before this moment. By the time we reached the car, fear had dissipated and delight was back. We agreed to ask family to pray, but there was no need to tell everyone and get them all stirred up about nothing.

Thus, we began the attempt to strike up a friendship with the mammoth notion that we would be parents. We found ourselves caught in a quandary between two opposing ideas of which many fledgling baby-makers grapple. We were intensely aware that we were about to be outed, naked, and on display, our incompetency just waiting to be announced to the world—the very ones we had as of yet endeavored to convince otherwise.

How exactly does one prepare to be a mother? A father?

It was my own mother that provided a lone morsel of assistance during my months-long hunt for parental insight. This seemed the unlikeliest of sources to me and surely must have been the first baby step toward the proverbial coming-of-age role flip, through which I come to see my parents not merely as fountainheads of embarrassment but prudence as well. Upon my ramblings of self-doubt regarding the tyke to come, she offered the window into reality that had helped her gain the confidence required of parents.

"I just looked around at all the idiots raising kids and said, 'Well, if *they* can, then *I* can.'"

And for reasons unknown to me, reflecting on the collective stupidity of all humanity and the sheer volume of birthed humans allowed me to sleep better.

There is a competitor emotion that battles the inadequacy monster; one screamed at me, another whispered. Despite ourselves, we could do this. We could parent *this* child.

THE NAME GAME

An unintended consequence of not finding out the gender was the realization that we now had to agree on twice as many names—one for a boy and one for a girl. Other than consensus on avoiding the entire genre of *Pat* monikers—the ones that could be assigned to either gender—when it came to names we were not getting anywhere. You just don't want to mess this one up and unknowingly place a permanent burden on the one you gave birth to. It seems wise to cut down, as is possible, on the arsenal of reasons to hate you before you have even held him or her. The recent surge of cringe-inducing names given to celebrity offspring does nothing to help, because you know they thought it was a good idea, and who's to say that your good idea for a name is not better suited for a dog than a person?

It *is* a big deal. By what means will people beckon this one? How will he introduce himself to persons whom he is meeting with a singular opportunity to make an impression? What designation will sit atop her résumé when applying for that job she really wants?

I have no idea by what means other people come to the name, but apparently we were not alone in our struggle as shelves were replete with naming books and web sites available by the dozens offering to help us land on the one name that would define a life from here forward. Only after purchasing and perusing does one realize that a list in book form, complete with names you would have never considered otherwise, only expounds the possibilities that already seemed overwhelming.

Gafna is of Hebrew origin, a name meaning "vine."

Thanks.

We began to develop our own system, hoping that somewhere along the way we would arrive at a sufficient designation. Celebrities had taught us that merely being guided by what we liked would not be enough. We decided to craft rules—*if-then's* that could be offset when the appropriate exceptions were triggered. These guidelines were derived by what we thought a name should or should not entail. Once these decisions were made, we pushed every possible handle through these parameters. What developed was some sort of naming funnel—such that names were cast off more readily at the bottom where the strictest criteria choked out almost every one.

- It could not be common. Our child would not be common.
- Neither could it be the first time it was used as a name.
- We were not doing the family thing; Ginny's family had run the gamut on this one, and so we were branching off.
- *Jr.* was out. Along with it went all names ending in *y. Ginny* had married into *Mooney*, and the "knee-knee" was too much for her.
- Syllables became important, as the whole name, if said at once—as it never actually is in real life—must sound as if it went together.

Ginny and I agreed that both parties had veto power. It seemed only fair that we both actually liked what we would have to repeat by the thousands. In practice, Ginny was always the proposer, and I was the one who vetoed every single name offered.

Quickly we became aware that our system was helpful but flawed—it produced only names that we did not hate but none that we loved. So we landed on making a working list of every name that could be a possibility. We added and subtracted and revisited it often.

Looking back, I think we did not want to land on a name just yet; we were having too much fun. The name game is a way we anticipate our children. We cannot see them. We are unable to hold them, but we can debate a name, and so Ginny and I discussed at length why that name wouldn't work for this one. This one was special, and the name had to be right.

NO HAMMER

Twenty-two weeks pregnant. Ginny loved pregnancy. Having heard many women speak of their own experiences in terms often reserved for plagues and wars, I encouraged her to keep this reality a secret from other women. Nighttime served for daily rundowns on how the day had gone: number of public gags, particular smells that induced nausea, and standard menu options that were suddenly appalling. Days were filled with stroller research, name-hunting, and nursery preparation. Against this flurry of baby fever, five weeks passed rather quickly, and we headed in for our second ultrasound.

The interim had also been filled with prayers to God asking that there would be nothing wrong—no cysts, no abnormalities—nothing. And in order to cover the bases in the off chance that there was something wrong, please go ahead and take care of it. These early prayers served as my introduction to desperation, as well as providing the initial insight into things dads do—the weight of being a father.

Because dads get stuff done.

Already there was a crib that had to be put together and pictures that needed hanging, just to name a couple items on the list marked *Matt*. I, unfortunately, did not possess the slightest idea of how to correctly do either of these, but in true father fashion, this fact did nothing to dissuade me from hammering away—pounding out unnecessary holes in multiples of five and piecing together parts without opening the directions.

The possibility of something being wrong with our child was a proposition in which I found no hammer to wield—a feeling of helplessness on a scale that was foreign to me, a limbo state where I could only hope but could not actually affect. The outcome was beyond me, and I hated that reality. I guess every parent hates that reality. I needed a hammer and a wall to clobber.

This appointment was not with Dr. Paige Partridge, the kind one I had almost allowed myself to like, so I bit my tongue and held at bay the hundreds of questions in my head to let this guy do his doctorly thing. Ginny lifted up her shirt as the tech applied copious amounts of belly jelly. There was baby with a quick heartbeat and hands around the face. Turning our way to provide an explanation to the wide-eyed couple studying his every move, his words conveyed thinly veiled optimism. Things looked good. The cysts were gone. There would be another ultrasound in weeks to come, but that was all. He asked us if we minded going to Little Rock next time—they had better equipment—just to be sure. "Sure" we said, unable to hide our excitement with the news of no news. If he had suggested it could help, we would have walked to Montana.

Four
THE WAY OF A WOMAN

1989. When I was twelve, the typical Friday night routine found me at Crystal Palace Skating Rink lacing up rented skates—the ones fashioned from tan pleather, complete with the unnecessarily bright orange rubber mallet glued on the tip, a design seemingly inspired from some combination of highway barrels and Rudolph. Of course, this must have been just as purveyors of skates would have wanted it, because everyone who could afford to do so bought his or her own skates—sleek, real suede, with multicolored wheels.

The skating rink was the elementary equivalent of the antiquated American pastime of cruising. For the young and uncultured, *cruising* is driving cars up and down the same road for hours on end. Of course, we were more than willing to trade muscle cars for wheeled-boots if it meant obtaining what at the time felt like cresting Mount Everest for a preteen—independence. Crystal Palace was one of the few places our parents were willing to drop us off, unsupervised, for hours at a time. So this warehouse with a snack bar became my classroom for many things other than the Hokey-Pokey. Somewhere in between the limbo and free skate, with background vocals provided by Tiffany, I was schooled in the ways of women.

All I had wanted all semester was for Ali Friddle to give me the time of day. She had transferred to our school, ushering with her that nebulous feeling that no twelve-year-old can articulate, but we all know. And whatever it was, none of the other girls in the class possessed it. And Ali knew it. She chose boyfriends at will, each gleefully answering the call. Like the farm ball left-fielder hoping for a call-up to the big leagues, I waited. Lacing up my skates that particular night had all the makings of the most epic slice of my short life. Earlier that week Miss Friddle had started returning my attention, and within minutes we were "going together."

I had skated with girls before but never a girlfriend. With the lights dropped, a teenage employee announced that the next song was couple skate. I appeared calm, just savvy enough to pretend that I had not been waiting for this all year long. Sliding off the carpet, we stepped onto the shiny wood-grain floor hand in hand, passing many of our friends who headed in the opposite direction to sit in booths—alone.

I cannot recall how many revolutions around the rink were made before *the moment*—just not enough. Shifting my weight to the outside foot in order to begin the necessary leftward turn, a corner I had successfully maneuvered thousands of times on Friday nights other than this one, my ankle gave. I fought valiantly in the losing effort to remain upright and even released her hand in mid-collapse. I was down.

I gathered myself, disappointed in being completely fine—having hoped that I had broken my fibula or, at least, be allowed to brandish some sort of grotesque swelling—anything that would induce empathy rather than laughter. Mustering the courage to stand again, I could only watch her leave—the red triangle of her Guess jeans gliding away at a pretty good clip.

I found a booth and began to replay the moment in my head when it all went wrong, all the while fending off tears with the valor of a knight—boys learn early that emotions only get in the way and provide stockpiles of ammunition for the enemy. If there were any way the night could possibly go worse, outside proof of the inward implosion would be the doorway by which it came.

I did not cry. In the midst of trying to figure out how one becomes invisible, one of Ali's friends came skating over to my booth to inform me that Ali was breaking up with me. And just like that, the dream had become a nightmare.

This was merely the first pair of shoes thrown into the baggage I was toting when I met Ginny. As I look back, it is peculiar, if not pathetic, to analyze the criteria whereby I gauged a woman. Of course, she had to be "hot." And as shallow as it seems, that may actually be one of the few that would carry over to a new list if I were to start today from scratch. Let there be no doubt—Ginny is "smokin'," but time spent with her left me reshaping, adding, and evaluating what I thought I wanted—like taking a bulleted list to the grocery store and then stumbling upon an aisle you never knew existed. Upon discovery of such a magical aisle, you cram your cart full of things you did not know you wanted until now. I only knew what I wanted upon seeing it on display through her.

She approached the world with childlike wonder, asking questions and listening to anyone willing to proffer an answer, as if each person encountered had something of note to offer her. She was kind, with a compassionate heart in ways that I could not quite grasp but hoped I one day could. She had eyes that made me want to write songs. She referred to herself as a "new believer," but it was evident she did not "have religion." This trend carried from meeting to dating and into marriage, as now my list would be most simple to explain if you just knew her.

And yet not in meeting, dating, or marriage did I give thought to what type of mother the woman I sought would be. With child coming, this exclusion clearly seemed of nuclear proportion. From what I can gather of the gender, women take the fatherhood factor into account from early on. So this must come as a surprise to them—men do not. Or at least this man did not.

Yet five years into marriage, as my mind began to apply the motherhood question to Ginny for the first time, I had complete confidence. Having shattered all expectations and lists that I had devised thus far, I was sure she would do the same when it came to being a mother. She has always exceeded my wildest of wishes.

All of this I found while looking for a girl who would not skate away.

Five
A DAY NOT FORGOTTEN

Thirty weeks pregnant. On a day that was to most everyone else a typical one, the sun rose, traffic slowed at the predictable bottlenecks, people moved around in busy fashion—and our world was forever changed.

We had driven to Little Rock, passing time chatting about nothing and listening to Ginny's latest favorite band. I have no recall of the moments in the waiting room or of what the third ultrasound was like, although I know to us nothing was unusual, just revisiting sensations of the unbelievable ability to see through Ginny's womb and glimpse our child, as though looking through a window. But it *was* different—we were just unaware.

What I do remember is that after the baby show, a team of three trudged into the tiny room together, walking slowly, with heads down seemingly stepping through unseen wet concrete. And we knew not *what* was going on, just that *something* was going on. With a low voice and in sorrowful manner, he told us that "things had progressed" and abnormalities were evident: a hole in the heart, enlarged kidneys, clinched fists. He continued with his diagnosis, but I had quit following. His mouth was moving, but I could not hear him anymore. I strained to listen, knowing I desperately wanted the information he was giving. The mind does strange things to protect the heart.

I reentered the room somewhere around his explaining that all the abnormalities could be linked to a syndrome or alternatively could present stand-alone maladies. The only way of knowing which we were dealing with would come through an amniocentesis.

Ginny was asking questions. She had done some research in the interim and was aware of some of the worst-case scenarios. I had mostly avoided such information, as if doing so evidenced a crack in my battle armor of hope. It was Ginny who long before pregnancy had one day mentioned that she thought we may have a child with special needs—spoken in a manner typically invoked for conversations on the weather or lunch plans. I made a face, dismissing the whole conversation as quickly as possible. Now she was asking questions about syndromes, and I was crying—one of those surreal experiences I had only heard of before in which you watch the moment rather than live it.

Each word of their answers pounded as they reset and swung away again. It was not good. Desperately looking for any glimmer of a false-positive equivalent, they offered scant seeds of hope among a bountiful harvest of bad news. In that moment I hated them—desperately wanting them to be idiots and to have gotten it all wrong. They were the sergeant sent to the house to tell Mom that her boy was not coming back from the war.

In one moment the bearer of news alters your life; though nothing has changed in the particular moment, it is just that now you know what you did not know before they came. So you hate them and simultaneously recoil at the thought of being in their shoes.

Apparently having blown people to bits before, the trio made decisions for us—a couple suddenly unable to process anything other than the news they had just delivered. We were told where to spend the night and that they would arrange for us to see a pediatric heart specialist in the morning because there could be in the future a need for open-heart surgery. After more discussion they left the room to let us be alone.

There was nothing to say. We ducked our heads in a hug, each trying to lessen the load of the other while overcome with weight ourselves. To those in the waiting room, I guess we looked much the same upon our exit as we did on arrival, but nothing was the same. Having entered the room as expectant parents, reminding the ultrasound tech that we did not want to know the gender, we walked out as shells of the couple who had entered.

We arrived at the hotel and decided to call each of our parents—ongoing reverberations of the shrapnel spread to us that day. They listened. And they cried along with us—aware that no words would suffice. Walking aimlessly to a restaurant, we attempted to formulate a plan—because when life hits the fan it feels good to have a plan, nailing down the few things you can control.

Our new friends back home had planned a surprise baby shower for Ginny upon our return. I had been let in on the plan in order to help pull it off. Calling Heather, Ginny tried to tell her thanks but that the shower needed to be canceled or at least postponed. She began to sob, unable to get the words out. I took the phone to complete her sentence but also failed, choked up in an attempt to cancel our first baby shower. Despite the lack of words, Heather understood the underlying message. She cried with us and told us she was sorry and that she would be praying.

NOW WE KNOW

Upon arriving home from Little Rock, we went to see Dr. Partridge. Among the many things that were still hazy was the question of whether or not to do an amniocentesis. There are serious but rare risks associated with an amnio; besides, we both knew the outcome would have no bearing on whether or not we would continue the pregnancy. There was no weighing of pros and cons. No discussion. What has since been questioned in terms of bewilderment seemed a lone spot of clarity in a period of perpetual blur—this was our baby.

The test would confirm whether or not there was a syndrome or whether all of the abnormalities were just unrelated issues. Paige gracefully explained that if they were unrelated, then doctors would set about to treat each one and that this was the better of the two options. Alternatively, if the various anomalies were related to a syndrome, then there would be nothing that could *fix* the syndrome, and we would need to decide what measures we wanted taken. And by way of nuance, she made clear that implications of a syndrome were of a more serious nature in an already-serious discussion. So we did the test and were sent home to wait on a call that would tell us what measure of hope to have.

Ginny answered the call in the kitchen and sat down at our long wooden table. I took the seat beside her, watching, looking for clues in her mannerism. She was calm—and sad. Paige had opted to make the call herself. She told us it was a syndrome. It was "Trisomy 18." The call was short. What else was there to say?

I don't think anyone actually knows how he or she will handle that mysterious moment in life when such a reality comes his or her way, but we've all played it out in our minds at some point, maybe many times. Folks have since taken time to let us know that they do not think they could go through what we did. This strikes me as odd due to the fact that they seem to have placed us on some pedestal—beyond them. I take the preceding conversation in stride and as the compliment they intend to give.

But this is merely self-protection on their part. They want me to be in a different category. They want to believe they are unlike me, that I am closer to super-hero status than they are—I am strong, and they are weak. Of course, what can be seen plainly from my angle is the unspoken subtext that runs through their dialogue: *Things like this are reserved for those who can handle it. And because I could not, I am safe.*

I do know what else they seek to convey. They mean, when they have played it out in their heads, they are unable to advance the storyline beyond this moment, unable to get their heads around the reality that their child may not make it. *That* part I get, because I still haven't gotten my head around it either.

FAITH WHERE HOPE ONCE STOOD

Thirty-one weeks pregnant. One extra chromosome.

Stooping low, I dropped down directly in front of the crib on both knees, collapsing until my forehead rested on the newly laid rug. I writhed and reset, making futile attempts to find comfort in this posture. I had meant to pray, but words balked where thoughts ran wild.

It takes so little to change the course of life. Many times it is the smallest things that leave wakes sufficient to overwhelm the mighty, and certainly the fragile. Nuclear bombs get headlines while single lumps, outsized by marbles, rip mothers from homes, leaving behind bitter husbands and new adults where kids once stood. Moments such as these shake in an instant the foundations laid throughout a lifetime, causing one to question and probe everything. I had busied myself fending off the colossal only now to be overwhelmed by an adversary outsized by a single strand of hair.

Upon hearing the words "Trisomy 18," we had both instantly developed an insatiable hunger to know everything this mysterious diagnosis encompassed. Information, while incomplete and unhelpful, was available in volumes. It was a genetic defect but not hereditary, occurring at the moment of conception, but no answers as to how one is stricken—a fact that seemed particularly cruel, leaving us with no one to blame, not even ourselves. We were looking for the cure, but there was no mention of such.

Trisomy 18 is also known as Edward's Syndrome, which seemed a bit too friendly a name for what we were finding out. The explanation started off with a basic biology lesson that I'm sure I had sat through many years before, a kid unable to imagine ever needing to know this level of technicality.

At conception the chromosomal makeup of mother and father combine to provide the new life with twenty-three pairs of chromosomes; each pair is comprised of one chromosome from Mom and one from Dad. At least that is the way you hope it happens. Apparently there are all kinds of genetic disorders that do not follow the script.

The chromosomal pairings are numbered one through twenty-three. On the eighteenth pairing in each and every single cell of our child, there existed three chromosomes, where there should be only two. This minor addition affected every aspect of a life.

We scavenged for facts—for something to hold fast to. But shared traits, possible outcomes, and percentages were the only things proffered as concrete, and each of these seemed grim and black as night as we desperately searched for any illumination.

Many with the disease are undiagnosed—miscarried prior to birth. In fact, the chances of making it to this earth alive with full Trisomy 18 are less than fifty percent, and if this unlikeliest of events does occur, you are left needing another miracle, as the life is often one of hours or minutes.

Thus, aware of what one additional chromosome wrought on our child, we were unaware of what effect it would have on each of us. Ginny was ten weeks from her due date. A day that recently could not come fast enough suddenly quickened pace, approaching at blinding speed. Each second, each kick now presented an invaluable gift. If absence makes the heart grow fonder, then forecasted absence makes the heart aware, awakened to the expansive beauty in graces previously held common.

Suddenly our lives were typified by paradox and contradiction. A quick glance offered up a couple preparing to usher in new life. A baby was coming. Crib sheets and bath supplies were needed, as were finishing touches on the baby's room. But a steady gaze instead revealed activities not customarily undertaken by expectant parents. Researching strollers gave way to searches for crafting a detailed outline of what medical measures we wanted undertaken on our child's behalf.

And people were starting to tick me off.

There is no way to hide pregnancy. It is as blatant to the checker at the grocery store as it is to your own mother. Everyone makes his or her standard comments—the ones meant to acknowledge, even celebrate, a new life on its way. Everyone assumes—with the baby bulge accompanied by the familiar waddle—that he or she knows how all of this unfolds:

The gal scanning your groceries at the checkout counter asks if it's a boy or a girl, following up your answer of unknown gender with a joking rant questioning your sanity. You don't tell her that you just want to hold him or her, regardless.

A probably good guy tells of how his two little girls are driving him crazy, advising us to enjoy the time we have before that little monster arrives, because life is over after that. And you have to agree—life does seem as if it may soon be over.

The mothers share all their unsolicited advice on products, feedings, and everything else, trying to play sage but unknowingly leaving you ill—as you hope desperately for an opportunity to put any such advice into practice.

They do not know, you tell yourself, *and should not be despised*. It is you, not them—increasingly apparent that you are no longer suited for the world around you as daily standard affair and procedure leave you breathless.

So Ginny and I learned, through patient attempts to inject our reality, to instead go along sometimes. It was too tiring to attempt to fix their perspective, and seemingly little was gained by waging the battle. Slowly we accepted the reality that ours was atypical, and such requires an explanation not owed to the world, that things—as they perceived them—were not our reality.

I think this is when we stopped trying to fit in.

For us, the necessary preparations were mostly unseen—movements of the mind and heart trying to fathom the possibility of an end. Greetings and good-byes are not meant to be simultaneous propositions. *And how*, we wondered, *do we go about preparing to say good-bye to a child we have yet to meet?*

As the earth shifted beneath us, there were but precious few things upon which we landed. Our faith surfaced through shared acts of desperation. For us, walking away from faith was not a viable option. I fear that this revelation may resound of strength and resolution, but in reality it is quite the opposite. The thread that held us tight to faith was our profound understanding of our own weakness—for where else did we have to go?

And so Ginny turned to Scripture, and I to prayer. She dwelled on the promise and security of His never leaving, while I attempted to get His attention. In my prayer times, there seemed to be two options available to me as a believer, each justified in Scripture but polar opposites. There were two distinct lenses as I, on my face in the nursery, talked to the invisible One on behalf of the one to come.

I could accept this tragedy as my lot in life—passing through the hand of the only one able to change things, for it is He who is in control of all things, sovereign and at work in every good gift and terrible occurrence. I could resign myself to an inevitable outcome, and my prayer would be that He be near us, not to overwhelm us, and to fulfill His claims in our time of need. And I prayed that.

Despite how plausible and appropriate such a prayer seemed, I was unable not to append a cry for more. And so I did. My life of faith in Christ told me to believe—against rational leanings otherwise—that God was able and that He actually requested me to ask of Him the impossible, all with the believing heart of a child.

He would have to tell me no, and it would not be for lack of asking if He refused the answers that I sought.

With the newly purchased rug beneath my knees, I cried out, begging for healing or misdiagnosis—any miracle would suffice. I asked that this nursery be needed, prayers lasting for long stretches but containing very few words.

Please let us know this child.

PLEASE PRAY

Somehow we managed to spread the news we did not wish to deliver to unsuspecting family and the closest of friends. It was always difficult and awkward, never any easier with practice. We tried to anticipate questions in advance and answer accordingly, but the truth always managed to weasel out despite our attempts at coherency: we do not know.

Those around us had a decision to make. Would they incorporate our tragedy into their own lives, or would they watch at arm's length under the guise of giving us space?

Friendships, still forming, and thus far centered on shared meals and shallow conversation, were vaulted to a land far beyond where they would naturally have found themselves. In an instant, our lives were overshadowed by pain on the horizon, and we, in unspoken manner, assumed to travel this path alone, understanding of anyone who did not want to make this trip—one that we ourselves sought to avoid if at all possible.

In such moments, the inner need for others, for community, for a tight-knit crew to man the ship, is blatant and obvious. Yet there is an opposing, unseen pull—a force that longs just to be alone.

It quickly became apparent that just as we ourselves did not know how to enter the tidal wave approaching, those around us knew even less of what to do with the news. At just the moment you need to lean on those surrounding you, they look back with blank stares—willing but unschooled on how to best prop up your ever-increasing weight. So we began to lay out breadcrumbs—clues as to how we should be handled.

As we communicated a message of the proper posture to take when dealing with our new reality, we found folks grabbing for the script we offered—readily admitting that they did not know what to do or say but thankful for our guidance.

However, we still had a large contingent of folks to tell: friendships we had carried from childhood, those in the various places we had called home, and the ones we had just not run into since our world had exploded. It was an overwhelming proposition to sort through those you actually make the effort to tell and those you hope find out. Call them up out of the blue? Start with small talk, or dive right in?

There were reasons we felt it important to get the word out despite the fact that the entire proposition made us physically sick. We had a deep desire for the prayers of anyone who would do so on our behalf, and we had an innate yearning to communicate accurately the way we were approaching this child.

So I started a blog.

This would get the word out while simultaneously not requiring any actual interaction. The plan was to point our friends to it and ask for prayer. Our feelings would be there for viewing by anyone who wanted to do so. You would not have to wonder, we would tell you..

FRIDAY, JUNE 09

What We Want You To Know.

Posted by Matt Mooney at 5:11 p.m.   6 comments

Ginny and I think it important that people understand where we are coming from and how we are approaching the days ahead:

1. *There's nothing you can say to make it any worse or any better.*
   We know it is difficult for our families and friends to know how to comfort us or what to say to us. Therefore, be relieved, and know that your presence, phone calls, and support are what we need, and just the fact that you show us you love us *does* make it better.

2. *We're praying for a miracle.*
   We are praying (and ask you to join us) for healing. We are praying for life for this baby. We know beyond a shadow of a

doubt that our God is able to heal our child. And in the same breath, we know that He is worthy no matter the outcome.

If you do want to pray with us, here is what we would ask you to pray for:

1. For healing.
2. For life and time with this child.
3. Most important, that God would equip us for the days ahead and give us the strength to say, "Not our will, but your will be done."

3. *We are excited to have our first baby!*

We could not express how important it is for you to understand that we are not in despair. Rather, we are excited to have this baby at this time. This is our first child, and we cannot wait. Of course, we would do anything in order for this baby to be healthy, and we have cried enough to last a while; but we feel the Lord is sovereign, and therefore this is the baby for us. And we anxiously await our gift.

4. *We do not know if it is a boy or girl.*

Again, Trisomy 18 has not changed our approach to our first child, and we really do not know the sex.

5. *We're not strong.*

If you happen to think we are handling this well (and there are many moments I would argue that point) and see any strength in us at all, please know it is from our Father and not due to anything having to do with either of us.

6. *What can you do?*

Pray for all three of us.

MONDAY, JULY 03

Update

Posted by Matt Mooney at 4:05 p.m.   3 comments

Thanks to everyone who has written, called, and prayed. We cannot express how appreciative we are to you all. We continue to seek your prayers. Folks have let us know that they appreciate the information and would love to be updated. To that end, we anticipate updating the blog as information is known. Again, thanks.

Dr. Visit

Today began the cycle of doctor appointments each week. The appointment went well. Everything is moving along just as hoped. We have been told that we will have a baby by August 1 (Ginny's original due date).

Good News

In the good news department, Ginny and Baby are continuing to grow (this is especially good for our situation). Also, each week that passes is closer to term, and many times these babies come early. We are also thankful for our doctors, who have been great throughout.

It is a comforting thought to us that prayers on behalf of this child have risen and will rise up to our Father.

WEDNESDAY, JULY 12

July 11 Update

Posted by Matt Mooney at 12:49 p.m.   0 comments

Doctor Visit

Today we had the second weekly exam. All went well, and not too much has changed. Although, of course, delivery could come at any minute, the doctor seems to think that everything is progressing, but "probably" not this week.

We go to the doctor again on Tuesday (July 18). We continue to pray and seek the Lord. He continues to give us all we need for each day.

We'll continue to update as baby nears.

Thanks again for your prayers, calls, and notes. We continue to hope.

TUESDAY, JULY 18

Baby's Coming!

Posted by Matt Mooney at 9:28 p.m.   28 comments

That's right, everyone. We will have a baby on Thursday (if not before). We went for our weekly visit, and Ginny had progressed to the stage where they want to go ahead and induce on

Thursday (July 20). We are super-excited and cannot wait to meet her or him. We've got names, we've got a baby seat, and we've got candy bars for me to stuff down my throat in hopes of warding off fainting.

We would appreciate your continued prayers and anxiously await the culmination of many petitions to our Lord.

Many folks (in close proximity) have asked what we want them to do in regards to visiting us at the hospital. We want everyone to know that we would love to see them. However, with this birth come many unknown circumstances, and our wishes will be determined by the outcome.

All that ambiguity to say—we would love for anyone to come to the hospital who wants to—just understand that seeing us or the baby is not guaranteed. While we would love to share our newest addition with everyone, we may need some time to ourselves.

Thanks for joining in our excitement for the miracle that is this baby.

Updates will follow. :)

During

PART 2

II'S  A BOY

July 20. I held Ginny's hands and stared into her eyes, making my best attempt to look confident and resolute, desperately refusing to acknowledge the purple and pink spots, apparently seen only by me, bouncing all around the room and multiplying quickly.

Did I eat breakfast?

She was shaking and shivering, fearful of the procedure going on behind her. She had decided to go with the epidural in hopes that it would provide the best opportunity to be alert and present in the moments directly after birth, as these were possibly the only memories we would possess. I was just trying to stay upright.

Needle. Needle. Don't look back there. She needs you. This is the biggest day of your life. Stop thinking about the needle! Needle. Needle.

All the staff at the hospital seemed to be on the same page. I'm sure I was not supposed to be privy as to how it went down behind the scenes. To me it should have appeared seamless. But our friend Josh—while snooping for information—had overheard Dr. Paige giving instructions and a pep talk of sorts to all the staff, filling them in on details and imploring them to be ready, because "today was going to be hard, but special."

We had attempted to prepare our family and friends for the statistical likelihood of possibilities that we would have only minutes to share with this child—and if so, then it was possible that each of them would never meet him or her. Telling grandparents that they may not get to meet their grandchild seemed selfish, but we feared the scenario whereby we would miss our own time with this child in an attempt to make sure that he or she met everyone else.

Attempting to set our minds on hope, we were, however, constantly faced with decisions that required thinking through worst-case scenarios. In a strange way, creating backup plans that kicked in only if our dreams were shattered became second nature. Questions surrounding the condition of the child seemed to drown out all the typical ones associated with the fact that Ginny was hours from delivering a child into the world. I am not sure how much thought either of us had given to the mechanics of the actual labor, but it was certainly less than it would have been in light of a normal pregnancy. And so, having not given much thought at all to an epidural, Ginny was visibly scared. It was over as quickly as it had begun, and she was lying back down now, hastily creating a mental checklist of additional things that she may have failed to prepare for.

Ginny had created a playlist for this day. It was carefully crafted, full of low-key songs—some peaceful, others upbeat, and many with undertones of desperation and worship. As the songs looped through their rotation, a hospital room—with hushed staff scurrying in and out—transformed into holy ground; there was a palpable feeling that *something* was about to happen. However, no one yet knew the appropriate reaction, only that the anticipation contained portions of both fear and wonder.

Weeks before delivery, Ginny had found herself driving back from a trip to the grocery store, pleading with God in a manner that until recently she had never known but had now become commonplace. In a desperate plea, she banged on the steering wheel and begged God to "unclench the fists" of the little one within her. She wanted a healthy baby; the fists were merely a starting point. Wiping away tears and trying to keep her focus on the cars around her, she repeated her request, only more loudly and with more pounding, a rising crescendo of intertwined hope and despair aimed at bending the ear of the One she knew heard her the first time.

In the afternoon it became clear that those around us were moving from a posture of waiting to one of action and preparation. Ginny and I prayed together in the breaks between checkups and guests, asking for life and hearts prepared for what was to come. I raided the rations that had been stowed to keep me upright amidst the nursing bra and a tiny white gown, carefully chosen by Ginny as the first outfit. I chose the Snickers and tore into it, packing another into my pocket just in case backup was needed.

The time was now.

"It's a boy, you guys!" Dr. Paige proclaimed as she hoisted him to Ginny's chest for a brief introduction; just as quickly, he was whisked across the room to the neonatal team for attention. I followed my son, trying to read the team's gestures and faces as to how he was faring.

Ginny was across the room, asking Paige if he was all right.

"He's crying! That means he's breathing, right?"

Paige did not look up, continuing her work on Ginny and sobbing, not equipped to answer the barrage of questions from this new mother. To no one in particular, Ginny was making a mother's declaration:

"His name is Eliot. Eliot Hartman Mooney."

Men and women attempting to gauge his breathing and vitals surrounded Eliot. I could not get close, and I was unable to see him. I held the camera above my head and over the shoulder of someone tending to him and pushed the button. I remember thinking that this might be my only chance to get a picture of my son alive. I took a short look at the image and then put my eyes back on the doctor.

The team dispersed, and the doctor carried Eliot back to Ginny. He explained that he was breathing and that he wanted to take him to the nursery in order to "continue analysis." These basic words of the doctor were to us the most beautiful syllables ever strung together—the code we had agreed on during preparatory meetings with the doctor that would indicate that circumstances did not appear immediately dire.

Our friends and family in the hall had been informed that we had a baby boy but were still waiting to hear anything else. I emerged from the room carrying Eliot, wrapped in a blanket, and joyfully proclaiming to an awestruck and tearful room of folks, "Look at my son!"

They returned him from the nursery with additions—some stickers and an IV. I hated that they had given him an IV, and while understandably necessary, the viewing of such seemed to blunt my celebration. Ginny was doing her best to feign patience as she reached for him with arms wide open the minute the nurse brought him back into our room. We were briefed that Eliot was doing surprisingly well; his six-pound frame was considered large for his condition. The nurse unwrapped our son and tediously explained every unique facet of his body, as well as the things they had done while he was away. Ginny listened and studied every inch of the boy she had borne, reveling in finding things the nurse had not noticed or at least did not mention.

With unsure but delicate movements, she now pulled away the hospital-issued blanket, allowing just enough slack to view him from the waist up.

His head was perfectly round.

Arms were thin, and his frame was long.

He had hair—a lot of it—brown with a reddish tint and more of it in the back than the front.

All his hairs came to a point on his forehead——a widow's peak like mine.

His eyes were almond-shaped, and eye contact revealed a child who seemed to look right through me.

His left ear was unformed. A protrusion of cartridge existed where the ear would have been, appearing as if his body just gave up working on it at some point.

Tenderly foraging for his hands, she smiled upon discovering each of them.

Both fists were clenched, although each in a unique manner.

On the right, his thumb overlapped his pointer and middle finger, while the left was a bit looser with the pointer finger permanently angled at a half bend.

She would later recount that these tightly-formed fists were the most beautiful hands she had ever laid eyes on, and if given the chance, she would not change a single thing about the hands that she prayed against just days before. Tiny hands, deemed abnormal by this world, were suddenly our new ideal—harbingers of the incalculable ways that our world was to change.

The heels of his feet were prominent with each big toe set lower than the others.

The second and third toes on each foot were webbed, and the left two were completely joined.

He was here, and he was perfect.

Family and friends funneled through for an introduction to our surprising little one. The air was thick with reticent exuberance, everyone hopeful but silently afraid to leave. As visitors finally waned and went home after a long, tense day, it dawned on us, just as it does with all rookie parents, that we had no idea how to care for any baby, much less this one.

Of course, he was staying in our room for the night. The new nurse introduced herself to us and let us know that she had been hand-chosen because of her experience with babies who needed some "extra attention." Eliot was hooked to various machines that monitored oxygen in his blood, heart rhythm, and various other metrics. If and when any of these measurements fell above or below a certain window, they would beep an alarm.

Knowing nothing, upon the frequent signaling of these maddening noises we looked for assurance from the staff or called the nurse, peppering a list of questions as to how concerned we should be. It became apparent that we were not the only ones disconcerted by the alarms. About an hour into her shift, the facade fell as the new nurse broke down sobbing.

"I am not the nurse for this baby." Words heaved between sobs. She was apologetic, seemingly waiting on us to kick her out the door in disgust.

"Oh," I said, managing but a syllable.

Awkward silence hung in the air as even I was curious to see what I would say. Somehow, through unspoken marital understanding, these types of situations always fall to me for response. Ginny, the nurse, and I awaited a reaction.

It was by now the middle of the night, and the hospital was dark and quiet. She was scared, and that was common ground where we could meet her.

"Well, we disagree."

I began picking up the pace as I now had at least an end point even though I still did not know how I was going to get from here to there.

"Ginny and I have prayed to God for months that He would orchestrate every single detail of Eliot's life. And here you are. And so you're perfect. You're an answer to our prayers. Besides, our hope for Eliot's first night has nothing to do with you, your competency, or your feelings."

We all hugged, and she went back to work. I took a breath as she left, looking to Ginny for affirmation that I had said the right thing; she never looked my way—too busy locking eyes with another prayer answered.

Propping my reclining chair beside Ginny's hospital bed, we smiled and recounted the unbelievable events of the day. Ginny had done splendidly. Her smile had not wavered since 4:59 P.M., the time he was born. All night long we never put Eliot down. It never dawned on us to do so. We handed him back and forth between ourselves for the entire night while the other one slept. I wanted to remember every moment this night held and decided that watching ESPN together at three in the morning sounded like something fathers do with their sons, so we did. The night was at times horribly scary, but it was the greatest night I had ever known, and all I knew was that my prayers would now be a plea for more nights like this one.

TUESDAY, JULY 25

Eliot Hartman Mooney

Posted by Matt Mooney at 9:27 a.m.   69 comments

Born July 20, 2006, 4:59 p.m.
6 lb., 18-1/2 in.

God has answered our (and your) prayers. Eliot is a four-day-old miracle. Thanks to all our friends and family for their help and support. We are all doing fine and loving life.

We are currently at the NICU, where Eliot is doing well, and every day is a new adventure for us to treasure. We would love your continued prayers for Eliot's precious life.

Updates are tough, because every hour is spent at the hospital, but we'll try to keep them coming.

TUESDAY, AUGUST 01
Happy Birthday to Eliot
Posted by Matt Mooney at 2:07 p.m.   32 comments

We wish there were more time for us to share the many things we have experienced with sweet Eliot in the last eleven days, but there just isn't enough time between feedings! We celebrate Eliot's life and the miracle God has given us in him each day at 4:59 P.M. with a birthday party. Today he will be twelve days old! Each day is amazing, and we are loving being parents and seeing the many answered prayers. Please continue to pray for us as we prepare to go home—possibly tomorrow. We are asking that you pray specifically that

1. We would not live in fear.
2. Continued life for Eliot.
3. All the details of transitioning home.

Thanks.
Matt and Ginny Mooney

WEDNESDAY, AUGUST 09
Home Sweet Home
Posted by Matt Mooney at 11:08 p.m.   4 comments

Oh, my.
Well, Ginny and I have broken down, and for the first time in five years of marriage, we have cable television. We also now

have Internet. Therefore we will be updating the blog more often so everybody is in the know on Eliot's life and in the know on how they can pray for him. WE PLAN ON UPDATING EACH WEDNESDAY (so there's some help to those who have been checking every day and getting mad at us).

Update

We have been home a week now and must admit that, although Eliot often asks of the whereabouts of his NICU nurses, we have loved being home. We packed up today (oxygen and all) and went for a big outing to the pediatrician. It was the first venture out for Eliot since being home. He did splendidly—sleeping and being cute as usual. To mark the occasion as well as introduce Eliot to the finer things of life, we headed to Starbuck's for a Mooney family outing. It was great, and we thoroughly enjoyed the hint of normalcy—the fam goes out for coffee.

Eliot's Care

As far as care goes, Eliot is on oxygen and is fed through his feeding tube. His feedings are timed in order not to feed him too fast. Each feeding takes an hour and a half (preparation, feeding, and so on) and he eats every three hours. That's right, quick mathematicians—that's feeding or getting ready to feed for half of the day. It's really quite simple, and he is able to do whatever while he is feeding. Mom and Dad have had a crash-course lesson in nursing and parenting and have loved the chance to learn how to best take care of Eliot.

Thank You

Ginny and I cannot begin to express the gratitude we have for each of you who have showed your love to us and our son. Letters, gifts, meals, visits, blog posts. You may never know how much you all have encouraged us. Thank you. Most important of all, we have been encouraged by the vast numbers of people praying for Eliot. We've had reports of prayers rising on behalf of Eliot from New York to L.A. and even Russia, believe it or not. We continue to need and ask for your prayers.

From Here On

People have asked if Eliot is better or if the doctors have changed their tune as to his surprising strength and condition. The simple answer is no. Therefore, each day is truly a miracle, and we have experienced multiple miracles along the way. He has a laundry list of complications but continues to surprise. Therefore, we ask for healing, continued life, and grace to see life as our Father does.

At some time in the future we hope to share with you all what Eliot has taught us, but for now we continue to enjoy each minute and be students of his precious life.

Matt & Ginny

WEDNESDAY, AUGUST 16

Sitting Beside Grace

Posted by Matt Mooney at 12:35 a.m.   75 comments

I am sitting beside Eliot. We are almost halfway through his 11 o'clock feeding. Mom is asleep, and the best part of my day has begun. My feeding shifts are late night/early morning. She takes over around 4:45 A.M. and cherishes her mornings with her son.

What a week to update you on—there are one million joys to report, and rather nothing to report all at the same time. Eliot is doing great. Going out has now been practiced and perfected by Ginny; thus, Eliot has been for a stroll around the neighborhood, out to eat twice, and even made it to his first church service. His many expressive faces have been memorized, and we are now able to interpret their meaning with reasonable precision. Eliot is seldom upset or crying; his rare frustration centers on working his bowels.

We are utterly humbled by the continued prayers of many. We ask for them to be continued. It is fun to hear how Eliot's life has reminded, taught, and inspired so many.

Well, I promised to share that which we have been taught by Eliot. Here is just a fragment of the lesson. Ginny and I have both been struck by the fact that the fulfillment of our deepest desires is often found in areas opposite the places we were looking. Truth be told, Eliot's condition is the type of thing that many (us included) fear and hope against.

However, whose joy surpasses ours? Down a road we would not choose, we continue to find unspeakable joy. Truly, the Lord's ways are not our own. Joy and sorrow side by side. If you have a chance, please do this for us—please post a comment. It can be as simple as "Hi, Eliot" or maybe a written prayer—whatever floats your boat will suffice. Make sure to include your name. We think it will be fun to see who is following Eliot as well as hear what you have to say. So, even if you've posted before and even if we do not know you, we would like it if you post something to let us know you are out there. Thanks.

Well, I do believe I smell an odor I have come to recognize as of late. Better go change a diaper.

Matt & Ginny Mooney

WEDNESDAY, AUGUST 23

Full of Surprises

Posted by Matt Mooney at 3:12 a.m.   15 comments

Well, I've got one hand on the pacifier and one typing. Wish me luck.

This week brought with it some great memories and milestones for the three of us. Eliot's feeding has been stepped up, and he has responded splendidly. Also, he has become quite fond of his pacifier (thus, the five-finger typing project).

Ginny has noticed that he begins to pucker about five minutes prior to feeding time. What a kid! Another surprising development has been Eliot's playfulness with the toys attached to his seat. Most every time he is put into his seat, he stares long and hard at the objects in front of him; he then reaches out and taps them. At first, we thought we were being naive and that there was no way he meant to. However, he has proved us wrong as he repeatedly performs. That may fall in to the "things only a parent can appreciate" department, but we were overjoyed.

Ginny and I are loving every moment. I have decided not to go back to law school for the semester and am considering a part-time job in the afternoon. Ginny is looking forward to possibly easing back into making jewelry. However, truth be known, we have both cleared our plates in order to enjoy the life given to us.

In the way of memories, many were made. We'll share two that stand out. First, the three of us walked (and rode) to the park a couple of blocks from our house. About a mile out from home, and without warning, it started to rain. Gradually, the drops progressed to what must have been the hardest rain of the summer. At first Mom and Dad were a little shell-shocked, feeling as if we had the "awful parents" award in the bag. But a funny thing happened. We pulled the handy cover completely over our son and had the time of our lives. We laughed, found cover, then opted to get soaked and take it all in. Eliot has a knack for turning the potentially frightening into fantastic.

I must apologize in advance, for this next memory will not be done justice by my words. Eliot turned one month on Sunday. (Hands down—favorite sentence I have ever written.) Early in the day Ginny and I talked of how we wished we had invited a lot of people over in order to celebrate. We wanted the full birthday experience for him—the whole nine yards. We decided to forgive ourselves since things had been a tad bit crazy and resolved to make him a cake ourselves. About four o'clock in the afternoon, Ginny heard something outside our door. We were expecting a couple who had called to come visit. Ginny yelled back to me, "Oh, my—there are a lot of them."

Ginny grabbed Eliot, and the three of us met at our front door. There before us, outside, in the sweltering heat, were fourteen of our friends and six of their kids holding balloons and singing happy birthday. At the song's end, they all came in, bringing gifts and a birthday cake for Eliot. It was a real-deal surprise party. They released thirty-one balloons to celebrate thirty-one days of life for Eliot. People were everywhere, Eliot's friends were crying, and all hands were grabbing for cake. It was beautiful chaos. When it was over, Ginny and I sat together crying, discussing how not a soul would ever know the significance of that event in our lives. Only the Father could have crafted such a gift. Thanks, friends. You'll never know . . .

Updates on Wednesdays. Please continue to pray. Thanks to all those who posted last week. We wake up each morning and read them. If you don't post, we don't know.

Seven
THE GIFT OF PRESENCE

I like to go eat with my dad. I love the man—
he typically pays, and I like that too. My father is gregarious, which has served him well
as he peddled insurance products for years to
people who are certain he is their best friend.
Upon introduction, one would fancy him
a Southern Baptist preacher; the world his
church, and the person in front of him at any
given moment this Sunday's visitor.

I recently picked up on a little habit of this man I have studied since birth. As he does so well, he took my whole family out to eat Mexican food. Upon being seated, he deduced that our waitress had not grown up in the great state of Arkansas and furthermore not in the United States at all. It was clear within mere moments that the extent of her English was limited to words typically reserved for waitresses in Mexican food restaurants: *water, salsa, burrito,* and so on. The rest of our table bridged the language gap by pointing to the item of our choosing and making sufficient eye contact until we were confident she was tracking.

But my dad would have none of it. When it came his turn, he chose to compensate for the language barrier instead by raising his voice to three times the amount of his already boisterous tone. He immediately veered the conversation out of her strike zone, inquiring as to how her day was going, what was her favorite dinner entrée, and what were her thoughts on the recent unseasonably warm temperatures.

She just smiled bigger with each inquiry, shrugging her shoulders and pretending to write an order down on her scratch pad. I pointed to what he wanted and smiled back. I had been a buffer many times before.

I've since noticed that my father's propensity to raise his voice in order to speak some universal language is not his tendency alone. For some reason, many humans seem to think that simply speaking louder will combat the problem faced when two persons not speaking the same tongue collide. But this solution does not solve the problem, instead often serving to exacerbate the issue altogether.

If grief is the art of grappling with a reality different than the one anticipated, then many Christians often yell at grief, speaking answers loudly to overcome the hurt they see in the eyes of another. But speaking, no matter the decibel level, is not the solution when hearing is not the problem. In fact, the very pursuit of a solution in the face of anguish is akin to solving a journey. Although you are trying, your efforts are in the wrong direction. A road must be walked, not an answer found.

In the Book of Job we find that this propensity of professed believers is not a new one. Job, unbeknownst to him, is the centerpiece of a discussion between the Lord and Satan whereby horrible circumstances are allowed to besiege the man described by none other than God himself as upright, blameless, and with no equal on earth. Job has watched his possessions, his children, and his health fall suddenly and inexplicably. As word of his demise reaches his friends, they come.

> Now when Job's three friends heard of all this evil that had come upon him, they came each from his own place, Eliphaz the Temanite, Bildad the Shuhite, and Zophar the Naamathite. They made an appointment together to come to show him sympathy and comfort him. And when they saw him from a distance, they did not recognize him. And they raised their voices and wept, and they tore their robes and sprinkled dust on their heads toward heaven. And they sat with him on the ground seven days and seven nights, and no one spoke a word to him, for they saw that his suffering was very great (*Job 2:11-13*, ESV).

Let's call Job's three friends *E*, *B*, and *Z* for reasons that include ink-saving and Hebrew language deficiency. They choose to enter within the pain of their friend as they sit completely silent for an entire week—a gesture of acknowledgment of the pain of a man they know and love. Well done indeed, friends of Job.

And then they open their mouths.

The next thirty-five chapters detail a back-and-forth discussion with the three men and Job as they offer up various attempts to pinpoint the source of the suffering that sits before them. As the three stooges propose to know the cause of Job's great distress, Job offers up defenses to attacks on his character, openly questions a God he still clings to, and freely criticizes the trio in a barrage of comebacks. Below is a sampling from Job:

He mocks at the calamity of the innocent (9:23, ESV).

I loathe my life; I will give free utterance to my complaint; I will speak in the bitterness of my soul (10:1, ESV).

Though he slay me, I will hope in him (13:15, ESV).

As Job reels, staggered with his new reality, the three appeal to their own wisdom as they question how Job could comfort others in the past but not accept dismay when it comes upon him. They appeal to having heard from God via words and visions dealing with Job's discretions—ones surely worthy of this reaction from on high. Much that they have to say is total truth, and each one takes time to praise the greatness of God; but truth pellets prove insufficient when sprinkled with lies and assumptions. A sampling from the so-called friends:

Blessed is the one whom God reproves; therefore despise not the discipline of the Almighty (5:17, ESV).

Know then that God exacts of you less than your guilt deserves (11:6, ESV).

Surely such are the dwellings of the unrighteous, such is the place of him who knows not God (18:21, ESV).

This is the wicked man's portion from God (20:29, ESV).

Agree with God and be at peace; thereby good will come to you (22:21, ESV)

Their words distill primarily into two black-and-white explanations that they offer up to Job in heaping spoonfuls. First, they encourage Job to bear it. Why must he rant and rave and seek answers? If he would only accept all that has come his way—his lost livelihood, the bodies of his children, the boils on his skin—then he would find what he sought. The power to get better was within

Job's reach if he would toughen up and accept this as his lot in life. Job just needs some good bootstraps and a strong tug to pull them up, all in his own strength.

Next, their pleas echo an inclination natural to many who happen upon the misfortune of another—you must deserve this. That is, the happenings of this world operate according to a formula whereby such drastic pain can be traced back to something that was done and therefore warrants the calamity that has come. Not only that, but it is merely a formulaic dance of counter-steps back to the good graces and favor of the Almighty. Again, this is your doing, Job, and by mere actions of your own accord you can correct all of this.

Scripture is replete with stories whereby one's trespasses do in fact result in the boomerang effect of sin and the downfall that comes due upon the transgressor. However, the fallacy of the friends appears when they apply occurrences as a rule for another. Scripture allows us to be privy to the goings-on in the heavenly realms before the fall of Job, and we know with full assurance that his tragedy was not the consequence of prior sin. Onlookers to pain cannot assume answers upon approaching another's dark night of the soul. Rather, we should come and sit and acknowledge.

After much volleying set on finding the origins from which such pain flows, God steps away from His onlooker status and takes center stage. When God decides to partake, He has words for all present. Job is not unscathed as He listens to God bellow questions that need no answers. But the larger portion of God's anger is reserved for the three who came to comfort Job.

> After the LORD had spoken these words to Job, the LORD said to Eliphaz the Temanite: "My anger burns against you and against your two friends, for you have not spoken of me what is right, as my servant Job has" (*Job 42:7*, ESV).

Job is commended; his friends are reprimanded. It is not good when God's anger burns against us. This is not a place we want to be. In a demand requiring mercy of an unjust nature, God informs Job that he is to make pleas for the forgiveness of his friends.

Throughout it all, Job attempts to understand the mystery of God. The three walking up the road attempt instead to take the mystery out of God, prescribing a predictable formula for a god living only in their own minds.

Job talked *to* God; his friends talked *about* God. The Almighty felt free to put Job in his place when he questioned and interrogated Him. God can handle our doubts and frustrations when they are brought straightway to Him. His wrath was reserved not for the questions posed by Job but for the misrepresentation of Him made by the friends.

What began with an admirable acknowledgment through silence of the pain of their brother stirred the anger of God when words and calculations came instead. They brought out formulas, presumptions, and advice, when what was needed was their relentless presence.

The truth of the friends is that they lacked faith. If Job was not responsible, then what kind of God does that make? If it was not a predictable formula, then how does God remain good or bring any good from a story such as this? Job clung to a faith that rang out louder than his wails of grief and questions for God.

For I know that my redeemer lives, and at the last he will stand upon the earth (Job 19:25, ESV).

A HOW-TO

The imagined middle ground: The night before we went into the hospital to deliver, Ginny and I headed to bed together and pretended, for the benefit of the other, to sleep. The more I tried to concentrate on lying still, the greater number of scenarios my unnerved mind generated. I was oddly relieved when the clock beckoned to start the day at 4:30 A.M. The time had come. We had made it to the delivery date, and I arose from my pretend sleep with clear prayers that all three of us would make it through the coming day as well. Ginny was being induced to ensure the necessary doctors and staff were present. I wondered if this chosen team was more skilled or simply the ones more ready and willing to deal with the potential realities of the day. My mind had played the scenarios of the nurses being briefed on our situation; I imagined them casting lots or drawing sticks to avoid being the ones who had to deal with us.

I loaded the car in silence. The city was dark and sleeping on the fifteen-minute drive to the women's hospital—the calm before the coming storm. I held her hand and affectionately patted her bulging belly. We were long past the stage where hugging was a real option. We had talked and prayed and planned incessantly for this child since the day of the positive pregnancy test so long ago; the dialogue had changed dramatically in the eight weeks since we had a diagnosis. On that drive it was apparent that all we had done was not enough. It felt as though we were stepping toward a fire as the heat dialed up with each passing second.

All the preparation and prayer were coming to bear in the hours before us. I popped the trunk as we pulled into a hospital parking spot close to the doors where we had been instructed to enter. As I lifted the luggage that had been packed weeks earlier from the trunk, a familiar voice from across the lot broke the eerie silence.

"Hey there, guys." It was Josh.

Unsure of when we were arriving, and knowing we would have held him off, he had ensured that he was our one-person hospital welcoming party by arriving at four and not asking for our approval to his plan. Upon his approach, a drip line trailed his every step, and I inquired as to why he was sopping wet. He just laughed.

"Well, just know the sprinklers here work perfectly fine. For crying out loud—who waters at 4:15 in the morning?"

The unwelcomed shower had left him looking for a towel as he walked the hospital grounds praying for us and this child. We were beaten to the birth of our baby by this faithful friend of ours.

If I had to describe Josh in one word I think I would land on *quirky*. His clothes are always impeccable. Years of working in retail left him unable to fetch the newspaper without looking as though he just stepped out of Ralph Lauren's closet. He is fiercely loyal, though that seems an understatement. If you're lucky enough to make it on the short list of folks he likes, then it's a lifelong designation and backed by his unspoken assurance that your life will be a good one if he has anything to do with it. He loves Jesus, but attempt to delve into a hot-topic religious discussion with him, and he will turn on you like a rabid dog. My bit of advice to those seeking to size up this man who has been my friend since childhood is the same every time: Don't try to understand him—just enjoy him.

There is often thought to be a middle ground for people who are dealing with those walking through suffering—a sought-after place of being available if needed, yet not obtrusive, a fringe position whereby one is able to be beckoned but otherwise not present. Josh knows no middle. Besides, this posture is a myth created and perpetuated in order to afford sleep to those unwilling to enter the suffering of another. There were no middle characters in our story—only those who jumped in and shouldered the weight alongside us and those who did not.

Josh stayed close outside our hospital room all day, asking each nurse who visited for the latest tidbits. Though the staff was initially put off by his insistence on a detailed update each quarter hour, by Eliot's arrival he had won them over one by one with compliments on their "nice earrings" or discussions on who it was exactly who made the horrid decision that everyone in healthcare should wear scrubs.

When Eliot was born and everyone cleared out for our first night with him, Josh slept on the floor outside the door, leaving only after a nurse's assurance the next morning that all was well and then to return in twenty minutes with boxes of donuts for us and the staff in celebration of Eliot's second day. Within the first month of Eliot's life, Josh was conveniently transferred to a job in Fayetteville. He stands by that version of the story, but we aren't buying it. Thus, his lessons on the value of presence continued.

Once at home with Eliot, I found that the most dreaded part of my day was always the same. The last stint of my overnight shift—2:30 to 4:30—was spent caring and cuddling with Eliot while Ginny slept. Half awake and lonely, I discovered that the silence during these times could go either way for me. Sometimes it served as a wonderful time of prayer and reflection on another day with Eliot; after more difficult days—the window of time was an enemy, tormenting me with fear, despair, and my own inadequacy to make things better for my son. During these times I would often hear a soft tap on the glass, turning to find Josh peering through the window—chocolate milk in hand. He had come to sit and talk and hold "E-bob," as he liked to call him, mainly because we hated it when he called him that.

We would talk and laugh and I would make him begrudgingly recount his day—replete with the normalcy of work and interaction that now felt so distant to me. Our conversations seldom hovered on any topic of a serious nature as we were both more fixated on our favorite resting little man than any conversation we could muster at such an hour.

However, one of these early mornings I do remember a conversation on the similarities between the scenario God faced and the one I found myself in. Somewhere between these wee hours and grappling with all that was tethered to my son, I offered up some pretty weird topics for conversation. I remember asking him how he thought God could send His Son knowingly or give Him up will-ingly and how *this* is the point on which we differed—God and I.

I asked him what he thought about it all, and I listened as he spoke. But try as I may, I cannot remember a word that he said. I only remember the gift of his presence in the hour of my anguish—walking the hospital grounds, outside our room on the floor with-out a pillow, tapping at the door with chocolate milk in hand.

HEAVY ARMS, HEAVY HEARTS

Heather and her husband, Paul, had quickly become some of our favorite Fayetteville folks. Within those first lonely weeks upon our arrival in Arkansas, they had made the mistake of offer-ing an obligatory hand of friendship. We grasped that hand with the sure-fisted fierceness of a desperate gorilla and did not let go when it all came crashing down around us.

They visited so often in our twelve-day stint in the NICU that they were now checking on the other children's progress on the floor as well. The hospital had allowed us to have a room, even though the NICU was not equipped for parents to stay overnight. Paul brought a mini-refrigerator, and Heather brought flowers, and most likely they provided all sorts of other items and services that I do not recall due to the blur of emotion and sleep depriva-tion that the NICU provided in ample portion. Both neonatolo-gists spoke broken English at best, but we had managed to com-municate in some universal tongue that we were not going home without our son. So they gave us the room directly across the hall. We took up residence with our mini-fridge, flowers, and family.

The room offered one twin bed, which Ginny and I shared. It was equipped for a patient, complete with a remote-control de-vice offering numerous reclining angles and touch-button access to the nursing staff. We would wiggle in back-to-back, making an attempt at rest, managing to get by on less sleep than we thought possible. There was no complaining. In months of pleading for divine intervention, not once did we think to ask for a king bed. Who could sleep anyway with him right there? Besides, on the rare occasion that one of us did manage to nod off, some nurse making her rounds insured our REM cycle never had a chance.

We often had to remind the nurses whom they were to care for—always checking on us, wanting to make sure we had slept or eaten that day, or wondering how Ginny was healing, as she had given birth just days before.

Periodically, the nurses took Eliot for some series of tests or checkups and informed us that we might as well rest for the next hour or so because we would not be able to see him while such-and-such was being done. It was these brief interruptions in our care of Eliot that made me realize how much life had changed in such a short amount of time.

These sequences allowed me to catch my breath above the waterline, only to long for the opportunity to dive down again. I *already* did not know what to do when not taking care of him. Once up for air and not busying myself with the care of my son, I would begin to grasp the gravity accompanying the situation in which I found myself.

In moments unable to predict, the weight accompanying Eliot's diagnosis and care wrapped itself around my neck and seemed to suffocate me, choking out the hope his life had brought and replacing it with fear. Slipping away to take a shower meant leaving the bathroom door cracked so I could hear Ginny if she cried out for help or the hospital monitors began to sound with their maddening chirps and beeps, screaming signals of something. It might as well have been yelling at us in Latin, because we never understood the meaning behind the frenetic concert of tones provided by all the monitors that accompanied our son, just the underlying notion that something was amiss.

The heavy load that started on my shoulders spread downward through my whole body, and somehow I intuitively knew that no one but Ginny understood the unique burden that had settled on me. Despite this understanding, the contours of what I carried were slightly varied from what Ginny shouldered. A mother's sadness has a look all its own; we quickly learned that each of us felt the weight at different times and in different ways. It was in these moments that those surrounding us on the fringes could sense the burgeoning gravity of our countenance and scavenged desperately for any way to accompany us or smooth the road that we were on.

Whenever Moses held up his hand, Israel prevailed, and whenever he lowered his hand, Amalek prevailed. But Moses' hands grew weary, so they took a stone and put it under him, and he sat on it, while Aaron and Hur held up his hands, one on one side, and the other on the other side. So his hands were steady until the going down of the sun (*Exodus 17:11-12*, ESV).

In this strange war tale, Moses headed to the top of a hill overlooking the battle that waged below. In a twist attributed to God, as long as Moses held the staff above his head, the Israelites won the engagement, but as soon as his arms lowered, the Israelites were pummeled. Friends of Moses, Aaron, and Hur came to his aid and assisted by giving him a rock to sit on and holding his arms up when he was unable to do so any longer.

Jesus, too, on His cross-bearing walk to Golgotha, was assisted by an onlooker. Simon of Cyrene was forcibly enlisted to help carry the cross of Christ to the place where He would be nailed to it. Those surrounding us must certainly have taken their cues from these unlikely participants gone before them. Though the burden was ours alone to bear, they did what they could—pulling seats and propping up arms. Though the battle was ours, they showed up to walk with us and share the weight of that which alone we could not carry.

Most assuredly, the best wisdom was displayed by that which our best companions did *not* do. They did not discount the burden that had besieged us or play spiritual charades in order to make it appear light. They acknowledged our position for what it was and entered into the lowlands we occupied instead of walking through the door prepped with answers. They willingly joined us on the road we desperately wanted off.

On that particular day in the NICU, the nurses had taken Eliot back for another series of tests, and Heather, seeming to pick up on the notion that time away from Eliot left us both afloat and in need of some direction, guided Ginny down to sit outside on the concrete benches just a few floors beneath the room where Eliot was being examined.

"I've been thinking, and I want you to know that Paul and I are in."

She spoke softly but with firm conviction. Noting the haze in Ginny's unrested eyes, she realized that her first approach had missed, so she delved further.

"We're going to walk this road with you. We have thought about it, and it is going to hurt, and as bad as I do not want to go—we're in. I wanted you to know that. Don't know where this is headed, but we love you guys, we are praying, and we're in."

These days we are inundated with inquiries that center on the same question. Someone somewhere will be facing a crisis, and one tangent to them—a friend or family member—will get in touch with me, inquiring as to what should be done for the person or what to say to him or her or buy for that one who is hurting.

"Was there anything that meant something to you—any timely words of wisdom or serendipitous activities that helped you during your time with Eliot?"

I want to say to pull up a seat for the person or lift at the elbows, but I know this is not what the inquirer wants to hear.

He or she wants more than I can offer. And I love the question, because it means there is someone wrestling in an attempt to walk a painful road alongside another and desperately seeks a way to help. Because all we humans can do when those we love endure suffering is to insert ourselves; so we show up bearing words, gifts, and actions. May this ever be—and all the more.

But I must admit that I hate the question as well, because in some it uncovers a flawed approach to grief and pain: *How can I fix this?*

I am unable to remember one verse that was quoted to me. Not one Chinese proverb stood out among all the rest. Of the hundreds of conversations I have had, not a solitary one enters my mind as the one providing the balm I so desired. Many people said and have said many things, but unfortunately only the few despicable ones seem to stand out. No gift comes to mind that comforted me in my time of need, and there were many.

Instead, I recall the faces—the faces of the ones who showed up with the gift, who spoke the words I cannot recall, the one who cleaned out our fridge. These I vividly remember. These I will never forget: the faces of those who interposed themselves into my pain.

Ginny leaned into Heather's shoulder with a ducked head and wept, unable to speak but hoping to convey that indeed she had understood the message. And just as quickly as the crippling weight had landed, it was but a feather lighter—a little less lonely as another chose to enter the very place we hated to be.

Opening the door on the day of Eliot's one-month birthday, I realized something for the first time. None of them knew how much it meant. Not Heather. Not Josh. Not these folks outside my door singing.

And try as I may, I always come up lacking in my attempt to let them know that I am not sure we would have made it without them. Showing up was just what we needed. Showing up was enough; it was all they could do. They did not provide a cure for our ailing hearts. In fact, it was a relief to see them *not* trying to achieve this end. They could show up and eat cake and manage to enter into the place that we occupied on that day.

In so doing, loneliness dissipated. They all brought gifts that day, not one of which I can recall; but they came to the door—with thirty-one balloons in hand, one for each day that Eliot had lived; they pulled us up a rock on which to sit and took turns holding up our weighted arms—and I still see their faces.

WEDNESDAY, AUGUST 30

Lordy, Lordy, Look Who's 40!

Posted by Matt Mooney at 1:22 a.m.   19 comments

This week brought more joyful memories with Eliot. Park trips, restaurants, and a lot of Mooney family bonding. Ginny and I are preparing for our first college football season with cable television. She is busy teaching Eliot the Alabama fight song while I threaten to purchase him every infant hog outfit in sight.

The week was not without its drama. One night during his 2 A.M. feeding Eliot managed to pull his feeding tube out. We had been warned that this was likely and even practiced the necessary steps to remedy the situation before leaving the NICU. Upon waking Ginny up with a yell, we realized that we did not have a stethoscope, which was necessary to replace the tube. We called Walgreens—they were out. WalMart did not answer. We decided we would drive to WalMart, and if they did not have one we would head to the NICU in Springdale. Upon walking out the door, I remembered that I had once—before Eliot was born—met our neighbor three doors down. She mentioned that she had heard of our future child's condition and that she and her husband were nurses. So with only having talked to the woman one time, I headed up their dark stairs and knocked on their door at 2:30 A.M. The husband answered the door, and after a little time to become coherent, he found his stethoscope.

Stethoscope in hand, Ginny went to it while I held Eliot's head still. After much wrestling, praying, and Eliot tears, the tube was down, and Eliot was able to feed. (I need to take this time to acknowledge that my wife is my hero.) This story makes it seem a little quicker and smoother than it actually was. The tube debacle did not conclude until about 6 A.M. With that said, this story is not told for any sympathy, but just because others have expressed that they want to know what was going on.

Trying to tell you what Eliot taught us is similar to serving grape juice as wine. More time is needed for the process. We are telling of a journey we are really still in the midst of. However, we can offer the glimpses that have been offered us.

Today we celebrate forty days for Eliot. I took the dog for a walk at Wilson Park in order to get out and enjoy the cooler weather. As I rounded the corner on my first lap, I saw it: a rainbow. Not the kind you *sort of* see and sort of don't; rather, it was large, robust, and could be seen from end to end. Initially I thought it might end somewhere around Hasting's, and debated going to look for it. The proverbial pot of gold could put a dent in some medical bills, you know. I thought better and kept walking.

> And God said, "This is the sign of the covenant I am making between me and you and every living creature with you, a covenant for all generations to come: I have set my rainbow in the clouds, and it will be the sign of the covenant between me and the earth . . . .
>
> Whenever the rainbow appears in the clouds, I will see it and remember the everlasting covenant between God and all living creatures of every kind on the earth" *(Genesis 9:12, 16).*

These verses make it seem as if God was the one who needed reminding, but I cannot help but think that it is actually us. God lifts the veil, reaches into the seen world, and places a sign—one to remind us of His promises, remind of His presence. I needed a rainbow.

Eliot is a rainbow all his own, a signpost to remind us of great things. As I look at my life, including four years of full-time ministry, I have no hesitation saying that God has used forty days of Eliot far more than anything I have said, done, or taught. *Why?* Because He wants to. Because God uses humble means for His glory. Eliot is a sign that is read differently by each person. To some he says, "Cherish the seemingly mundane moments of each day," to others, "Look and see the power of prayer," to still others, "Read how God does not work within the logic of humanity." All that through a child who feeds through a tube and has never spoken a word. What a kid!

So on Eliot's forty-day birthday, God provided a rainbow just as He did after forty days and nights of rain. You just can't make this stuff up.

Please continue praying for Eliot. We love posts. Thanks.

Matt and Ginny Mooney

eight
MARGIN FOR MYSTERY

I am naturally a rational being, an appetite served steady diets of lard during my years spent pursuing a legal education. So I cannot write about rainbows and not imagine readers expecting my next chapter to contain leprechauns, mermaids, and the like. I prefer to explain things in all their detail, to understand in entirety the world in which I walk, and to grapple with what I do not until question marks morph into periods. I, also instinctively, doubt others and harbor mistrust for most people I encounter. So I get it if you cannot buy what I am selling. I could not either if I were you. Except I lived it, and instead, I cannot deny it. I actually think God painted the sky on that day for me.

I now leave margin for mystery. Eliot ushered in all sorts of wild rainbow stories in multitudinous fashion. I am holding on to some of the others for myself. Not because I care what you would think—I moved beyond you long ago. I hold on to them for myself, because sometimes the flames tucker out when the burning escapes the heart in an attempt to decipher the elements of fire under the microscope of public scrutiny. God is alive and active in our world. And He comes near often in some of the worst times in our lives. He allows His coming to be discounted, but He still comes.

Ours is a world uncomfortable with mystery. With only sound bites from the political talking heads on the screen, I, and most likely you, have slotted them into a category in which I am aware of what they think about foreign policy, wealth distribution, and the right to bear arms. In addition to simpleton definitions of persons, over the last twenty years technology has produced a bombardment of data. If there is anything I do not understand, I am able to conduct a search that will almost immediately yield information sufficient to make me relatively knowledgeable on a subject I knew nothing about just minutes before. (Of course, the difference between information and actual understanding is a large one. Though via web search I may find libraries of data on Einstein's theory of relativity, it does not therefore mean I am any closer to insight.) However, this bourgeoning access to information coupled with notions of scientific advances may have served to lull us into a belief that someone somewhere understands each and every one of the very things I do not. To counteract this onslaught of input, I have developed ways to efficiently decipher, slice, and categorize all that comes my way.

But with Eliot I rounded corners to rainbows made for me. I had no explanation. I knew in that instant that some things in life are incapable of comprehension. Instead of reaching for clarifications or allowing my preset mechanism of deduction to take over,

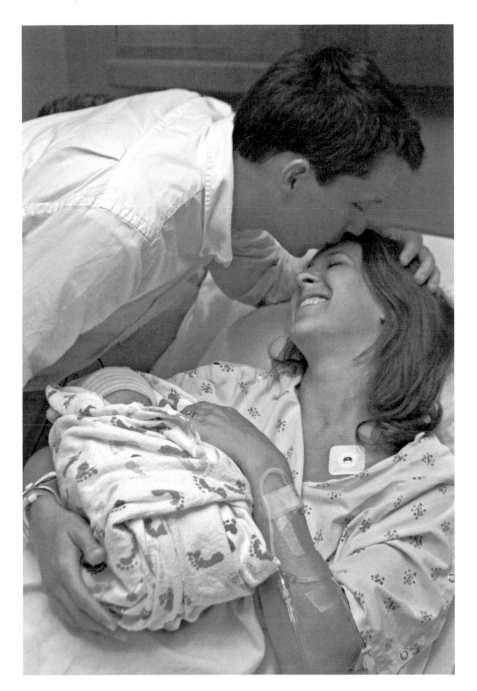

It's a boy! Ginny holds Eliot shortly after his birth.
I was proud of her and proud of him.

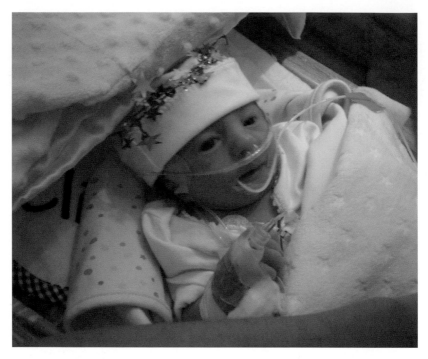

Eliot in the NICU. He is wearing his birthday hat fashioned by the nurse who joined in our first birthday party.

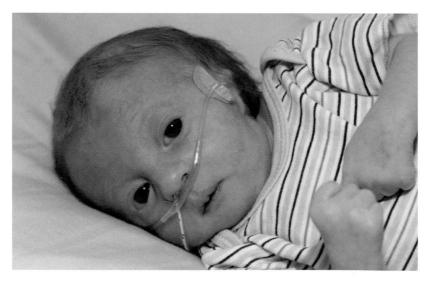

Cameras of all sorts were always within reaching distance. We took thousands of pictures of him. This is one of our favorites. But then again, they all are.

Josh snapped this picture of the three of us one night.
We asked him to stop taking pictures. He did not
oblige and we're thankful.

Eliot and I spent some significant
man-time on the couch. Ginny & I came
to cherish every aspect of Eliot.
His feet were just a piece of this
celebrated uniqueness.

We released 99 balloons at Eliot's funeral. One balloon to commemorate each day of his life.

This photo is shortly after we returned home
from Ukraine; Lena's hair has just started
growing out of her orphanage buzz.

We call them the rascals: Anders, Lena & Hazel.

This is a current photo of our family.
It's always a challenge to get everyone to look at the camera, but after numerous attempts we got this.

I began to see that claiming a relationship with the God of the universe is many things, but rational is not one of them. I was the biggest critic of my own developing margin for the inexplicable.

Many of us seem to spin our wheels attempting to make Jesus rational. Here's a quick review of some of the highlights of our faith:

- God created the world.
- There is only one God.
- Well, He is a trinity, but one God.
- He had a Son. This Son was God—and a Man.
- The world killed God—that is, the Son of God.
- With His death, death was actually overcome.
- He said that to follow Him you will need to die.
- Those who do follow will be persecuted on account of Him.
- Despite that, you will find true life only by knowing and following Him.
- If you completely understand *it*, then *it* most likely is not God.

How could God bring any scintilla of goodness from the sickness of my son? I do not know. I cannot see it. But I believe it—by faith. This acceptance does not mean I do not ask hard questions; but I allow for faith and mystery to fill in the cracks of His towering ways over my own.

Instead of a margin for mystery, it seems we are prone to craft God in our own image. Because we are all we understand. But I found myself thankful for the unexplainable. Hope springs anew from the understanding that I do not and will not—this side of eternity—understand all the nuances of losing my son. And understanding seemed a lousy goal in and of itself.

God has made much of himself known yet has purposely hidden some as well, reserving facets of himself for those who doggedly seek for more than a moment, as well as a portion of His being given only on the other side of this life. It seems to me that those outside of faith are not looking for us insiders to have all the answers that we often pretend to have. Rather, they are hungry for something beyond their comprehension. Jesus spoke in parables and seemed to purposely obscure much from those following Him. We hunger for the illumination of what we currently see only in pieces and shadows.

In the coming week countless individuals will line up and fork over hard-earned money to watch the latest, greatest two-hour movie. We will scour bookshops and land on a set of bound words and happily devote hours of our lives to digesting it. Movies, books, as well as other favorite escapes take us beyond the limits of our imagination. It is as though we are hardwired for greater things than many of us experience on this earth. These latent desires are evidence of an appetite for more. Our hunger is filled only when feasting on Jesus.

We point to Him with admitted mystery, revealing what He has revealed and acknowledging that He has not revealed everything. Others are drawn not only to our answers but also to where common questions find company. God gives answers. God gives mystery.

Our culture seems prone to hold nothing back these days. If I want to be known, I will blog, I will engage social media, I will tell all. I know that if someone pulls up the stream of information that is me—though we may not have met—I am known.

Having moved past the needless, uptight nature of the past, we have forgotten that some things were kept under wraps on purpose. Where once our thoughts and ideas were allowed to simmer and sit, we now serve up raw offerings in abundance without time of reflection. But there is a beauty in reservation. There is a posture that says I am here, but there is more to me than you can obtain in a glance. There is a mystery to all of us because we have taken on the nature of our Creator. It takes time to be known, effort to be known, and being known is always an ongoing endeavor. It is the same with Him. We are not our politics, not our status updates, and God is not encapsulated by a creed alone.

I now leave margin for the unexplainable nature of God. I acknowledge rainbows that were made for me. I have left the shores that felt so firm. Eliot's life would not let me sip drinks with umbrellas on life's beach. Through my son, God called me into the deep waters of His mystery and fullness. I still claw and scratch and demand answers, but I also sit and simmer and make a list in the waiting, one that I know will not be checked off until the shadows come fully into view in eternity.

TUESDAY, SEPTEMBER 05

Holland

Posted by Ginny Mooney at 9:55 p.m.   47 comments

At the end of last week Matt asked if I wanted to do the post this week. I said no. Then I thought about it and said no again. The second no was followed by him telling me he decided it wasn't a question anymore—he *wanted* me to do it. He doesn't ask much of me, so here I am, completely out of my comfort zone. To those of you who look forward to the eloquence of Matt's words each week, I apologize. Know that I, too, am disappointed.

This past week has been good. Not a lot is different. Alabama won, Arkansas lost. You know, the usual. There have been seven more birthdays observances, seven more days of rejoicing and celebrating and enjoying every second, seven more days of visitors and blessings. Eliot's biggest struggle is going to the bathroom, and we have been figuring out the best way to help, and there has been some progress.

There's no way to describe daily life, and even those who have had the chance to visit don't actually experience it. There are times when I look at all going on and think, *How did I get here? Wasn't I just in college? Wasn't I just walking down the aisle? And now I'm a mom. What happened?*

Then there are other times when it is the most comfortable and natural thing—as if God has made every part of my life up until now only a step in leading me to this—and as if I have always not only been intended to be a mom but to be Eliot's mom.

A friend gave us a short story this week printed on a piece of card stock about what it's like to have a special needs kid. Essentially, it said it's like preparing to go on a trip to Italy, learning all about Italy and hearing what Italy is like from all your friends who have been there, packing for Italy and getting on a plane to Italy. Then when you land, you realize the plane has actually landed in Holland . . . at first you are just surprised to be in Holland because you knew so much about Italy and not Holland, but from the second you step off the plane, Holland is not only incredible but better than Italy . . . and Holland actually becomes home.

I love our Holland. I love everything about Holland. I love changing Eliot's oxygen, I love that his food goes into syringes and into a pump and through a tube, I love his webbed toes, I love his whole right ear and his partial left ear. I love that the greatest accomplishment of my life is dropping a tube down his throat at 3 A.M. I love getting to see Matt be the best dad a kid could ever have. I love that so many unknowns have turned into forty-seven days of knowing every expression and cry and squirm and punching of the clenched fists. Though I am very aware that the unknowns continue, I am also very aware of the fullness and joy of today. God's goodness is not always packaged as we think; it's better than anything we could ever come up with.

Ginny Mooney

WEDNESDAY, SEPTEMBER 13

Posted by Matt Mooney at 2:26 a.m.   22 comments

Well, unfortunately for you readers, I—Matt—have returned to the typing. If you missed last week's post from Ginny, I suggest you read it. Have I mentioned that my wife is my hero?

On to the man.

Eliot continues to amaze and continues to find new ways to steal our hearts each day. He was weighed for the first time since his pediatrician visit. Drum roll please: seven pounds, three ounces. What a heavyweight! It is great to see him growing, and his food has been bumped up to account for his appetite.

Another fun Eliot-ism: we give Eliot his pacifier only when he is feeding. This is done to aid in digestion and allow him to associate sucking with his belly getting full. Recently ten minutes prior to his feedings he puckers up and works over his imaginary pacifier until Mom or Dad come with the real thing. Maybe all kids do this, but that's precisely the point.

Just a few items to pass along:
- If you're new to the site, you can check the archives for more information on Eliot's condition: Trisomy-18.
- We continue to be humbled by the prayers and posts and ask for continued prayer for Eliot's life.
- We try to provide an update and pictures each Wednesday.

Two-Month Birthday!
We continue to celebrate each day of Eliot's life with a birthday party, picture, and a prayer of thanks. Each day continues to be a miracle, and we are asking for many more. Two months of miracles is quickly approaching. Ginny and I have sought ways to commemorate the significance of a month. For Eliot's two-month birthday (September 20), we are asking whoever chooses to do so to send him a birthday card. Please, no gifts or anything like that, just a card. If and when you drop it in the mail, we ask for a prayer for Eliot.

As requested, we continue to relay the lessons gleaned from our son. The joy of Eliot's life is a resisted truth. We battled (still do), crossed our fingers, prayed, and fasted. You name it—I guarantee you we at least entertained the idea of doing it if Trisomy-18 could potentially be fended off. But without all that Eliot is, we could not experience all the joy that he is. And he is unspeakable joy.

Please understand that our prayers still go up to the God who can heal but whose faithfulness is not dependent on whether or not He does.

The truth will sometimes gag us. Not too long ago, as many of you already know, we had to drop a tube down Eliot's throat. Without the tube he could not eat. Needless to say, he coughed, cried, gagged, and cried some more. He fought us with all one hundred twelve ounces. However, we willingly gagged the boy we love so much because we love him so much.

We must watch that which we resist, because the hand of the one who drops the tube can be trusted.

WEDNESDAY, SEPTEMBER 20, 2006

Two Months of Joy

Posted by Matt Mooney at 1:28 a.m.   35 comments

Well, today—Wednesday, September 20—marks two months of Eliot's life. A cookout will mark the occasion. We've decided there is no way to adequately celebrate the joy two months of Eliot has provided. Ginny and I are so thankful that we know our son. We know his faces, we know his noises, we know that bath time and baby massage are his favorite daily activities.

Thanks to everyone who sent postcards. We'll post some pictures of all the cards and the birthday bash soon.

This week brought an all-new round of triumphs and challenges. Eliot has finally had more success going to the bathroom. After quite a bit of experimentation, he is doing much better in this department. Also, he has done well with his increased feedings and continues to add rolls faster than a Baptist potluck. Finally, after many dead ends, we were thrilled to find a food pump that better suits Eliot's needs.

Eliot has had a stuffed-up nose this week, which may sound inconsequential. But it has made some things more difficult. Breathing, feeding, and resting can all be frustrated by a runny nose. Feel free to offer up a prayer for the little guy's nose. With that said, Eliot is doing well and continues to amaze.

As you can see from the pictures, Eliot has managed to suck his thumb. We saw his desire to do so develop about two weeks ago, and we gave him a little help. Because his hand is clenched, getting the thumb actually in the mouth was quite a task. We tried not helping him to see what he would do, and although as you can see he sometimes thumbs his chin instead, he is figuring it out.

Eliot continues to teach, and we continue in our pursuit to pass on the lessons learned.

I must admit that until recently I have never longed for heaven. Don't get me wrong—it has always been somewhere I eventually wanted to be. It sounded great and all, but honestly, I enjoy the here-and-now just fine. I looked at heaven as through a telescope. It was a nice place, not too distant, the surface of which reminded me of my current surroundings.

Scripture describes the feelings that we as believers should have for the afterlife with these words: *longing, burdened,* and *groaning.* Whatever my affections for heaven were, these words would not be an apt description for them.

Enter Eliot. He is my reminder, my illumination. This world is out of kilter, not quite right. Eliot's head bobs with each breath. His heart has a hole in it. The list continues from there.

For the first time, I long for heaven. I want to be there. I want it worse than any desire I have ever experienced. This world will no longer suffice. I am restless for that which lies beyond.

Eliot has revealed the distance from earth to the afterward. He has taken my telescope and fashioned a magnifying glass—and the true distance from here to home has been exposed.

So that what is mortal may be swallowed up by life . . . .

We . . . would prefer to be away from the body and at home with the Lord (*2 Corinthians 5:4, 8*).

Matt & Ginny Mooney

Reminders:

*Updates on Wednesdays.

*If you don't post, we won't know.

*Please continue (or start) your prayers.

WEDNESDAY, SEPTEMBER 27, 2006

Closing in on eight pounds.

Posted by Matt Mooney at 3:22 a.m.   23 comments

Another fantastic week of enjoying Eliot.

We celebrated Eliot's two-month birthday last Wednesday. Thank you to everyone who took the time to send Eliot a card. He received over one hundred birthday cards. We had a small gathering to celebrate and spent the time together opening the cards and reading them aloud. Thanks.

Eliot also had his two-month checkup last Wednesday. He is a whopping seven pounds, fifteen ounces, and growing.

This week was as joyous as ever. The runny nose has cleared up for the most part, and with the bathroom problems seemingly a thing of the past, Eliot has been quite happy. There was the problem of seeing his mom so out of character—completely irate with Bama's lack of a kicking game. Luckily, Dad had prepped the little guy earlier in the day on what to expect when Alabama finally played a real team. Eliot has gotten over it, but I am not sure about Mom.

We have been attempting to live our lives as close to normal as we are able. I have started working a job that allows for flexibility. I am coping with being away, but I don't like it. Therefore, my workdays are short, and Ginny must give me a complete rundown when I get home. Ginny has been working a little as well and making trips out with her son. While life with Eliot becomes our new normal, we strive never to let any day be routine. With Eliot this comes easily.

Eliot continues to teach in ways this blog cannot contain.

Having a child has done things to me that I could not have imagined. Sure, there are the things such as smiling at every single child I come across and finding myself crying at cheesy songs I don't even like. But there's more. Eliot is the first thing I have loved as the Father loves me. He is the first recipient of my deepest affection that did not earn it. I have loved my family, my friends, and my wife, but each has won me over. Each has offered me something I deemed worthy of my affection. But not Eliot. I love him. End of story. I just do. I played a part in his creation, and I love him.

Sure, I receive so much from Eliot; but if I did not, my love would continue. Philip Yancey writes that grace is the understanding that there is nothing that you can do to make God love you more, and there is nothing you can do to make God love you less. Now I get it.

Ephesians 3:17-19 says it this way: "I pray that you . . . may have power, together with all the Lord's holy people, to grasp how wide and long and high and deep is the love of Christ, and to know this love that surpasses knowledge."

Matt & Ginny Mooney
Please continue to pray.

WEDNESDAY, OCTOBER 04

Birthdays, Bikes, and Baby Mullets

Posted by Matt Mooney at 3:31 a.m.   27 comments

Fayetteville was taken over this week by Bikes, Blues, and Bar-B-Que. The annual motorcycle rally brought in around three hundred thousand folks to the area. You read that right. Needless to say, we are not missing the rattling windows and deep hum that pervaded our neighborhood.

Not to say that BB&B was not appreciated by the Mooney family. Eliot was spotted twice at the rally—even getting his picture made with his stroller parked up beside a row of Harleys. His parents could be seen making sure no one lit a cigarette near his oxygen. Needless to say, his baby mullet allowed him to fit right in with the crowd. We have ranked this event as the number-one people-watching venue we have ever experienced.

Besides getting many "What in the world?" glances at the bike rally, Eliot continues to amaze. Birthday celebrations continue each and every day. We take a picture daily with the number of days present in the photo so we can keep track. Lately we have been attempting to spice up the photos with creativity.

Eliot continues to gain weight; this would most likely go unnoticed but for the numerous pictures we have of him in his thinner days. He will be weighed again this week, and we look forward to celebrating the verdict. His nose has been congested again. Changing his tube aggravates the situation, and we would ask you to pray, once again, for his nose to be cleared up.

Thanks again to all who have posted and prayed. We continue to be humbled by the support of others. I guess it goes without saying, but we continue to seek prayers.

I wish to convey a little more of the landscape of life with Eliot. For the sake of full disclosure and honesty, I must confess that there are many times my prayers are that the Lord would help me believe the words I write and say. The last few months have ushered in moments of pain and joy intermingled. Ginny and I have made every effort to focus on the joy, but the hurt and bewilderment have taken up residence as well.

We have heard repeatedly how strong we are, and we can only grin sheepishly and cut eyes at each other. We know we are not strong. We each know the tears and hurt of the other.

I fully expected at the outset of all of this to be mad at God—to have it out with Him. I've read enough of the Bible to know that He frustrates His followers and allows them to air their anger. But I am not mad. I am weary. Too dizzy to fight. I'm the boxer who does not know which corner is his own.

I doubt. I struggle. I waiver. And that's the truth.

So if Eliot's story has power, please know it is not us. I am thankful to follow a God who does not discard the traitors.

Matt & Ginny Mooney

WEDNESDAY, OCTOBER 11

Over 8 lbs. & 80 days.

Posted by Matt Mooney at 3:21 a.m.   15 comments

Another week of Eliot! He jumped up on the scales and proved what the pictures have been revealing all along. He tipped the scales at 8 lbs., 14. oz. This weight gain is quite an accomplishment.

Seven more birthday parties. Seven more baths. Seven more days with our son.

Eliot has quite a few new readers. Here are some pointers for the new folks:

- New posts typically on Wednesday.

- Check the archives in order to learn of Eliot's condition.
- Feel free to comment. We have been encouraged.

Eliot's life is always teaching, ever instructing, gently nudging observers to truth.

Our world is one in which we all strive for control. Everyone possesses a plan. Sure, some hang on more tightly than others, but to some extent we all desire to influence our circumstances. When something is wrong, we act. We do something to fix the problem. This all comes very naturally. If hungry—eat, if tired—sleep. You get the idea. Early on, one learns that his or her actions can determine the outcome.

This system works quite nicely, and I like the sound of it. It's so American, the pull-yourself-up-by-the-bootstraps, self-made man mentality that our grandfathers tried to pass on to us.

Everyone is afraid to admit that he or she does not have a plan. I love asking college freshmen what their plans are. They have it all mapped out. We crave control. At the least, we desire the appearance of being in control.

Eliot has managed to shatter our illusion of control. We can do nothing. Our utter dependence on the Lord is glaring. He's sick, so we take him to the doctor. The doctor can do nothing. It's a helpless, powerless place that we are in. But truth be known, this reality is where we have always dwelled. Eliot just helped us realize.

I am thankful that we know the One who controls. This is not always comforting. His ways are not my ways, and I want *my* way. All I can do is trust Him. And with Eliot I've begun to see that His ways are better and that He is worthy of trust.

> Where were you when I laid the earth's foundation? Tell me, if you understand *(Job 38:4)*.

This week ushered in both the lowest and highest points of our son's journey as of yet. We honestly are not prepared to reveal specifics, but suffice it to say that describing Eliot's life as a miracle just may be an understatement. Eliot is with us, and we are overjoyed.

Matt & Ginny Mooney

Nine
WHAT WENT UNSAID

I can now tell you what I could not bring myself to admit at the time of that blog post. We thought we had lost Eliot. Afterward I repeatedly pulled him close to smell him, asking my brain to please file this wonderful aroma—a union of baby, lotion, and oxygen—deep in the recesses of my mind, where it would always be available for recall. Each day of his life I made a point to behold him, painstakingly moving from his feet to his head, making note of each inch, absorbed in his presence like a newfound treasure— but even more so now.

His presence had always put life in slow motion and allowed each frame to be seen for the beauty it possessed. Now slow motion seemed cruel and hasty. Relishing each moment with him had become as natural as the next breath, and I remembered back to the first time he had this effect on us:

"Man, look at these stretch marks—can you see them?" Ginny asked, swinging her ample, eight-month tummy toward me.

"How about that?" I said, striving for complete ambiguity until I could be more certain of the feelings that accompanied her question.

"Are you still going to love me with these?" she asked with a smile, much in that way she does where she is half joking and the other half gauging.

"Nope." I said, hoping this tact would allow us to move on more quickly.

She didn't laugh but just glanced down at the bulge beneath her chest, caressing her stomach as if it were already a separate being. And I knew I needed to follow up.

"You know what? I am praying otherwise, but those marks may be all we have of our baby one day, and you better believe I love them."

Sometimes, although rarely, thoughts proceed from mouths where they were not born—ones you bear but are not the creator of. This was just one of those moments. Those are beautiful scars.

Such goes the genesis of losing and re-learning everything I thought I knew. Scars had never been beautiful before. And now, with him here, we were both as happy as we had ever been and as sad as we had ever known, all in the same moment.

I remember staring at my laptop that week, typing with the pained deliberation of an unwilling messenger. I wanted to give an update on progress and park walks, just like so many miracle weeks before, but the days making up this week would not let me do so. Struggling with how naked I wanted to be, I opted to drop hints that the last week was just as wonderful as all weeks had been with him, but unlike the previous weeks, it was also awful.

I had held him, one hand under his head and the other supporting his back, as he struggled that day. Ginny was pacing in circles of prayer, with dark stains on her shirt from ignored tears. Our minds, somewhere between numb and wildly crazy with fear, ran on autopilot—doing and saying the things we had unknowingly but apparently planned for the end.

But after some time he came back, tired from the battle but no less himself. And we somewhat rejoiced, having seemingly fended off our greatest fear; but there could be no true rejoicing with what we had all just experienced. Eliot had always been surprisingly healthy, and three months of unforeseen vitality had lulled us into a dream in which we were his parents and he was our son. End of story. But now it seemed we were being awoken to the rest of the story, that he was sick and his body was failing him.

I made my way to the shower unable to recall if I needed one or how long it had actually been since my last; it seemed as good a place as any for an attempted intermission from life. My life can be plotted by the places to which I escape. I always have a go-to, and it is always quiet. Ginny had made herself some breakfast and had Eliot in her lap; it all seemed just the beginning of another day, except that I wanted to die.

Turning the knobs slowly, I waited just long enough for the hot water to sting and stepped in, focusing my scattered thoughts as the water pelted my face, enveloping the tears.

I made a stab at coherent prayers, but the only thought I could muster was a bargain.

Me for him. Take me and leave him here with his mother. I reasoned as one facing pickpockets or thieves. *Please. I am not sure she will make it, and I don't want to be here without him. I'll do it.*

I am serious. Me for him. Please. Or maybe you could take us all. Anything but him—don't ask for him.

My shaking arms gripped my head, and I understood what it felt like to be crazy. Death was the ultimate failure as a father. I was now grasping for things I could do—any window for some semblance of control, and nothing was too outlandish if there were any way it could work. And dying in his place seemed the only chip I could come up with to wager.

So goes the beginning of losing my own life.

I stood still, watching the water run slowly toward the drain— my thoughts swinging intermittently between opposing philosophies and feelings, an erratic war with myself—full of slight advances and massive retreats. Having always heard of the miracles of Scripture—water for wine, burning bushes, loaves and fish— my hope for my own miracle was fading. Or worse, the divine intervention for my son seemed to be expiring too soon.

I could recall no template from Scripture for which to deal with *this* scenario. It seemed that the waters had been parted right there in our midst, and as we stepped out in awe of what God had done, the parted waters began to fall; the crashing waves were out ahead of us at first but closing in at a clip that made it apparent that we would be swallowed up by our own miracle.

I hovered over the drain, having not moved in quite some time; I felt foolish for thinking God could hold the waters back and questioned if He ever parted them at all. And on the off chance that He did, then I wanted to hate Him for refusing to hold them back any longer. I told Him I could never believe in Him again if He let me down on this one.

Then the pendulum would swing.

I know that you are faithful. You can still do this. I do believe. I know there is a miracle in the living room. Thank you. Please don't leave us. We need you.

Even in the better moments, the ones with normal breaths and less shaking, I could not bring myself to consider a third option—his faithfulness in our loss.

WEDNESDAY, OCTOBER 18

Almost Three Months!

Posted by Matt Mooney at 12:53 a.m.   20 comments

This week brought more wonderful memories with Eliot. He rooted on the Hogs at the homecoming parade and went shopping with Mom on Dickson Street. Best of all, we all got to go to a NICU reunion.

I have never seen my wife happier. I cannot portray the joy that I received from her glow as she showed off her son. She wrote about it for something else, but I think her words paint the perfect picture. So possibly against her wishes, I am stealing them to share with you.

Stick Horses & Surprises

Saturday was one of the greatest days I have ever experienced. Eliot was eighty-six days old, and Matt and I took him to the NICU reunion. It was a roundup, so we got to see the ever-so-serious neonatologists and sweet nurses from our twelve days in the hospital riding stick horses. Not only did we get to see them riding stick horses and dressed in their cowboy attire—we got to see the look on their faces when they saw that Eliot was there. I'll never forget those looks as long as I live. They were so surprised.

The logic of medicine says he should not still be alive, but he is. He's strong and sweet and such a fighter, and I felt that day the way I assume a mother would feel if her son became president or won the Heisman or developed a cure for cancer. If you had asked me in those days in the NICU if we would be coming to the reunion on day eighty-six, I would not have had an answer. All I had and all I have still is a mustard seed. My faith is not big—it is small; sometimes it feels smaller than a mustard seed even. But I am generally sure of what I hope for and sort of certain of what I do not see. God has taken that tiny glimpse of faith and done in

Eliot what really He does in us all: moved the mountain of death and given life.

Ginny Mooney

We hope to celebrate October 20, Eliot's three-month birthday, with a party in the park. As with all facets of life these days, the occasion is dependent on how Eliot's day is going. We have been asked to provide specific prayer requests. This we are more than happy to do. Thanks for all the prayers, and please continue to bring us all before the Father.

***Please continue to pray for life and healing for Eliot. We believe this prayer has already been answered many times and ask for more of the same.

***Please pray for Ginny and me. It is tough to specify what exactly to pray for. We now reside in such a strange land. Each time Eliot struggles or experiences an episode, we prepare to say good-bye and wonder if this is it. We are happy to live in this land, because here is where our son is, but it is unusual territory. Pray that we have peace, trust, rest, courage. Pray that the Lord will continue to be close to us. Pray that we will be able to live our lives without fear. Pray that we will sleep when we lie down. Pray that we will be faithful to tell Eliot's story, because it is a story of life and hope and one many need to hear. Pray that joy will continue to overwhelm us at moments we did not see coming. The Word tells us that when words fail us in prayer, the Holy Spirit communicates those prayers for us. These are the prayers we—all three of us—need.

Thanks once again to all who have prayed. We still love posts and draw much encouragement from them.

WEDNESDAY, OCTOBER 25

A Quarter of a Year

Posted by Matt Mooney at 3:25 a.m.   11 comments

Dad—10,630 days
Mom—9,860 days
Eliot—96 days!

A quarter of a year. That is how one friend described it, and we liked it. Eliot's three-month party was Friday, and what a party it was! Friends, pizza, kids everywhere. Can you beat it? Ginny and I attempted to address the group, but we each welled up with tears about a sentence into it. However, I hope the message was clear. Thank you, friends, for making this journey less lonely.

Eliot got his first ever cordless photos (no feeding tube, oxygen, or stickers). This was no small accomplishment. We had scheduled everything out to have them taken, but Eliot's feeding tube split the day of the scheduled change. We had to call our great nurse to change the tube immediately. The tube is changed every three weeks, so we tried to be all right with the fact that the photos were not going to happen. But we had been excited about them. Just as she was about to change the tube, our friend Brooke came in with camera in hand. The lil' man is quite photogenic. Thanks, Brooke.

We continue to fight fear. We continue to hope. We continue to laugh and experience joy. We continue to savor each moment with our son.

Ginny's twenty-seventh birthday is Friday, her first as a mom—thus, already the best one yet. Although the subject matter is different, I continue to recite the lessons drawn from a special boy.

I always thought Ginny would be a great mother—the kind who wore a smile through the chaos that is raising children and unintentionally made other moms feel inadequate, like seeing one reach her destiny. I always thought that she was strong, courageous, and able to weather whatever this world brought and that she would sharpen me and prop me up when I could not stand on my own—all the while acting as if she were doing nothing special. I always thought she was the clearest picture of Christ that God had given me this side of heaven. Needless to say, I thought a lot of her—and now I know. Thanks, Eliot.

Two are better than one. . . . If either of them falls down, one can help the other up (*Ecclesiastes 4:9-10*).

SATURDAY, OCTOBER 28

July 20, 2006—October 27

Posted by Matt Mooney at 10:39 a.m.   180 comments

Our fighter of a son has gone to be with Jesus. We celebrate his life and revel in the fact that he is finally well. We are sad. We miss our son. But do not mourn for us. Celebrate with us. Eliot's life points us all to worship. Join us.

> I have fought the good fight, I have finished the race, I have kept the faith. Now there is in store for me the crown of righteousness, which the Lord, the righteous Judge, will award to me on that day—and not only to me, but also to all who have longed for his appearing *(2 Timothy 4:7-8)*.

WEDNESDAY, NOVEMBER 01

Celebration of a Life

Posted by Matt Mooney at 12:12 a.m.   61 comments

Ginny and I, and many of our friends and family, gathered Monday to celebrate Eliot's life. It was perfect. Following a song titled "Everything's All Right," I struggled through the following:

> "Everything's All Right," not your ordinary funeral song, and "Don't wear black" are not your ordinary funeral instructions. But Eliot was no ordinary boy. His life was extraordinary.

> A dad speaking at his son's funeral is probably a little strange as well. But Eliot's is a story I must tell. Ginny and I have things to say, and I'm going to try to say them today. We also have a saying as of late which is "Go ahead and cry—we do."

> But if at all possible, hold it in for the next couple of minutes, or I'll probably lose it with you. I have a tag-team partner on board, so I can tap out at any moment. With that said, I apologize for reading. My communications teacher would be disappointed. But I am just gonna try to make it through.

> I want to thank you all for being here today. Ginny and I wish we could personally sit down with each one of you and express how much your actions have made our burden lighter.

Thanks for making a call when it had to be awkward for you do so. Thanks for letters and birthday cards for Eliot. Thanks for feeding us when food was the last thing on our minds. Thanks for a surprise one-month birthday parties and blog posts and law school softball tournaments for Eliot. Thank you to our family for your love and support. Thank you, Josh, Becky, Heather, and Paul, for walking through this with us.

Thank you all for joining us today to celebrate the life of a special boy who impacted so many. We view today as a celebration. We celebrate the greatest gift the Lord has ever given us. In Eliot we enjoyed so much. We loved so much. We learned so much.

Although Ginny and I had seats near the front of the class, you all joined in on the lessons, and the classroom kept expanding to include people we had never even met. We all sat in awe as God himself took a sick little boy and pulled back the veil to reveal lessons about himself.

An underdeveloped lung, a heart with a hole in it, and DNA that placed faulty information into each and every cell of Eliot's body could not stop the living God from screaming of himself through a child who never uttered a word. To an outsider it may seem nothing short of foolish to credit all this teaching to Eliot, but 1 Corinthians 1:18 says, "The message of the cross is foolishness to those who are perishing, but to us who are being saved it is the power of God."

It goes on to say that God's wisdom is unlike ours, and His tools are not what we would imagine. His tools are not the ones we would craft.

Not a pulpit, not a slick presentation, not a bestselling book but a six-pound boy with Trisomy 18—God found great pleasure to take a lowly thing in the eyes of the world and show Truth.

Every aspect of Eliot's life was a paradox. Because I hate it when people use words that I do not understand—let me define.

A paradox is defined as "a seemingly absurd or contradictory proposition that upon investigation proves to be true."

Truly, all of Christianity is a paradox. G. K. Chesterton writes that, "Christianity is a superhuman paradox whereby two opposite passions may blaze beside each other."

Our God teaches us—

- To become greatest I must become least.
- As a believer I have total freedom and yet strive not to sin.
- And ultimately I find life—in none other than the death of a man named Jesus.

Through Eliot we experienced the paradox of joy and pain ablaze side by side.

Truly, the Lord did not ask us to take a path that He had not already traveled on our behalf. Although we did not willingly give up Eliot, his life and death have given new meaning to the sacrifice the Father made when He gave His only Son unto death that we could have life.

And so today we celebrate. Eliot is well. And although we miss him more than we can express, we are separated from him only by our time left on earth. We anxiously wait to join him in worshiping the Lord.

Today we propose a new standard.

How do you measure a life? By years? By esteem

By productivity?

Eliot Hartman Mooney
99 days, 98 birthday parties—and today makes 99
18 nurses
17,557 visits to his web site
0 minutes unattended

Although these statistics are fun, they all fall woefully short of a metric with which to judge Eliot's life. We propose that Eliot's life be measured by impact.

Thus, truly his was a full life.

We encourage you today not to forget Eliot, not to forget whatever his sweet life taught you. Please go and do that which has been stirred in you through his life. And we look forward to hearing of the ripples he has made in eternity.

Finally, when you arrived you were handed a flower. We believe that Eliot's life is best understood when pictured much like the flower you hold. A flower is picked to be enjoyed, sweet to smell and viewed by all. When your flower was picked, a process began in which the flower's life will end. But this is not the way we view a flower. We just enjoy it. We take it in.

Thank you, Eliot. You were the joy of your mom's and my life.

PART 3

Ten
THE TASTE OF ASHES

The deafening silence was a daily reminder. The first few days after his funeral, I remember despising the haunting hush that fell over our home. Eliot's life necessitated a community and energy, and now there was only a void. Each silent moment was screaming that life had changed.

In a routine developed during Eliot's life, Josh often drove by our house without stopping—driving in circles to pray for the three of us. He sent text messages to inquire if we needed dinner or anything at all while failing to mention that he was making loops just outside the window. In the days immediately after Eliot, he was back at it. Upon approaching our house, he stopped cold at the sight of no lights within. Minutes passed before he realized we were both in bed—something he had not seen for months.

He later confided that this was the moment it hit him the hardest. There were always lights on with Eliot, because someone was always preparing the syringe for a feeding or holding him on the couch as he slept. But now—no lights and no sound. Just the still darkness of a normal house where only sunsets before, *normal* was nowhere to be found. Each day passed without celebration, each running into the next, untallied and unnoticed. We were learning to live again while feeling anything but alive.

As I cracked open the door coming home after a brief outing to the local bookstore, I heard what I hated. Ginny turned away at my entrance, trying to go unnoticed while wiping the evidence from her wet cheeks. I sat down beside her, desperately trying to avoid my typical response. This interaction was beginning to feel like my life's adaptation of the movie *Groundhog Day*, and an inaudible voice was reminding me to tread lightly as my recent attempts to help her had only served to make it worse. She did not speak; she only pointed in the direction of the canine cowering in the corner.

Less than two months after Eliot left us, Christmas came. I remember wishing we could ignore it, but try as I may, I could formulate no plan that worked to this end. International travel to Santa-less countries seemed the only viable option, but with new hospital bills appearing daily in our mailbox, I could not afford to get us anywhere that would not have mistletoe. We reluctantly decided to participate in the observance, knowing that decorations and gatherings would bolster the reality of our first holiday without him. Having opted in to Christmas, I mulled the seemingly impossible task of getting Ginny a Christmas gift.

I typically love crafting surprises, but the timing of this holiday took away the fun, putting me on mission for the gift that could do what no other gift could do. Although my penchant for surprise may sound quite cute and harmless, I can take it too far. While well-meaning, this habit has progressed to the point at which I am no longer sure the element of surprise is truly for the recipient rather than for me. I *love* to give surprises, and Ginny is typically a willing target for my pastime. She enjoys gifts of most any shape and size and has at least led me to believe that she does appreciate my propensity. For the most part, my hobby of surprise has culminated in her happiness, even when I have boldly taken what is by most considered a *couple decision* into my own hands for the sake of surprise. I think she liked both the cars as well as my choice of our first two homes. Tah-dah!

I decided I would surprise her on this Christmas with a gift from my heart. I knew just the thing—a perfect gift for the lowest point in life either of us had ever known.

I got Ginny a dog.

Why? I can't say. Grief does terrible things to a person, and this gift provided the greatest evidence of its impact on me. My wife had never shown an affinity of any sort to any animal as long as I had known her and, in fact, had quite a substantial furry-phobia due to being attacked by a dog in high school. She had been bitten so badly by a friend's family pet that the father, who had witnessed the attack himself, injured his hand by the blow landed between the teeth and jowl of a dog who never bit anyone again. This fact was made certain the next day when a lethal concoction ended Winston's life as soon as the vet opened the doors for business.

Armed with these facts, I thought it best to buy my wife a short-haired Wheaten terrier. I had done the necessary research for a fail-proof surprise:

- The breed's hair never stops growing, but it would not shed.
- It was large enough to exercise with her but not so large as to intimidate.
- It was not so small as to elicit neighborhood questions pertaining to my manhood when I took it on a stroll.

Needless to say, this gift *did* manage to hit the sought-after target of surprise. She even briefly feigned excitement while harboring a secret hope that all could come out well if the dog slipped out the back door and into the street through no fault of her own. After all, how could she be expected to shut the door with her hands so full of groceries? This way, I would still be able to believe my Christmas surprise was a hit, and she would not have to spend the next few months cleaning up dog feces at a time when just getting out of bed seemed like a win. Her plan for the dog's demise was foiled, however, as Wilson—the name she gave him—was terrified to venture past the back door steps when left outside.

When we had envisioned the possibility of great loss, it was a scene replete with tears and immense sadness. However, our forecasted mourning fell woefully short of the reality we found ourselves in. We would never have predicted that losing our son would make us feel certifiably crazy—seemingly unable to encounter a routine day engulfed with emotions that burned beyond our control.

In my ill-advised gift, Ginny found something to blame, continuously insisting that the *dog* was the problem. I rationally explained that there was no way any dog could account for what this one was being credited with, but this fail-proof argument of mine only served to further deflate the woman I loved.

And this to me was indicative of the most frustrating aspect of our shared grief. In the precise moment when all I wanted to do was lessen the load that visibly buried my wife instead, in a display of the effects of my own grief I only made things worse. Daily adding my own baggage to her heavy-laden shoulders, the inverse was true as well. Her attempts to ease my pain often served to cut me deeper.

Outsiders and observers are convinced that parents who lose a child are on the fast track to divorce. Many quote a mythical statistic that basically sticks its tongue out, coaxing you to save your energy and go ahead and file the papers. Possibly just paranoid, I remember feeling in public that others were weighing our words and body language toward one another just looking for the opportunity to confirm their suspicions that our marriage was struggling.

Although I hated feeling like a marital peep show, I fully understood why our marriage was being scrutinized. Valid statistic or not, the strain on our marriage from losing our son was unknown territory for us and left us in a perpetual state of confusion as to whether we should talk out the latest iteration of frustration or chalk it up to despair and let it go.

Our marriage up to this point had been five years of something beautiful and enjoyable for us both. Without a doubt, we had encountered the friction inherent in soldering two persons into one flesh but had managed to escape much of the embittered disillusionment often birthed in the first years of union. We found it quite simple to like each other and busied ourselves seeking ways to be together more often.

Now our alliance seemed more like something to navigate than enjoy. Somewhere along the way I remember calmly telling Ginny that it was all right that our marriage for the first time was "not fun." Though difficulty was the reality, not for a moment did we believe this time in our life would be eased by being apart. The only thing more daunting than working through our individual grief together was the idea of doing it alone.

Each of us found in the other a lone ally in the battle we were facing, and although on occasion we mistakenly wielded our weapons at each another, we never wavered in our knowledge that *this* was about *that,* and friendly fire was something to be avoided when possible—because when your child is ripped from this earth, you are just mad, unwittingly looking for somewhere to unload your hate. Those around you become targets, even though you need them as never before.

So just in case, we set up an appointment with a woman at our church who was a counselor. Carrie had just started taking appointments again due to her ongoing battle with pancreatic cancer. She was visibly sick, but her words packed the punch of a prizefighter. In her I met my match and was immediately drawn to this feisty woman who had no qualms at putting me in my place. I walked in the door of our first appointment telling her that neither of us were *sure* that we needed counseling, but we were *sure* that we did not want to be the couple too proud to darken the door of help. I made sure to mention that we were broke, and requested a timeline of visits and costs for fixing us. She laughed, kindly asking me to bring in my own timeline at our next appointment and that she would be happy to stick to it.

We were able to have only a precious few appointments with Carrie before her sickness relapsed, eventually taking her life in the days that followed. But the visits served as a starting gun for Ginny and me on the marathon race to regaining the marriage we desired.

Apparently Ginny did not need me to fix it for her and just wanted me to listen. I wanted to make it all better. But I began to accept my own ineptitude—choking the impossible desire to solve it. Slowly I began to allow room for outbursts of irrationality, because somehow the anger inside must get out, and this process is typically anything but rational.

"Yep," I stammered, placing my hand softly on her back as I brushed away her tears. "What did that dumb dog do this time?"

CURTAIN TALK

While marriage was the first stronghold of our former life to be tested by an onslaught of emotions, it was certainly not the last. Coffee shop visits, grocery runs, and routine meal preparation were all unwanted reminders that we now had in bulk the unwanted free time that had been scarce with Eliot present.

Within the spiraling throes of loss, basic realities and trivial details often disguise themselves, and in a cruel twist on the well-known proverb, life's sheep put on the skins of wolves as daily affairs became daunting. Eliot's life and care had quickly and joyfully become our reality, and his absence allowed for activities and errands that were prohibited with him here. The sheer fact that our arms were empty and able to be employed elsewhere made us loathe the activity itself.

In many ways, sadness ages its inhabitants. Suddenly I was groggy and unable to stay focused on the most menial of tasks, often opening my computer, then forgetting why I did so. In true form of an old man, I had no desire to small-talk. This, of course, presents a problem to the outside world already grappling with how to approach the one who recently lost his son. But I did not care. All conversations and streams of thoughts veered off the natural road into the median and onto the street leading up to the residence where my mind was trapped inside. Although I instinctively knew my civil duty to steer others away from the debris field of my pain, I allowed them to end up nowhere else.

"You ready for football season?" someone would ask, innocently attempting to wade into conversation.

"I guess—what do you mean?" I posed, not helping them at all.

"Well, you got Razorback tickets this season?" he continued, pushing through my first barrier.

"Nope. I was hoping we would be taking care of Eliot and unable to attend. You?" I was sensing the end now.

"Yeah. Hey, so sorry about that."

"The lack of tickets or losing my son?"

"Umm, the son part. Well, I'll see you around."

Game. Set. Match. You really want to talk to me?

Then there were the unaware whom I still felt no sympathy for.

"You guys have children?"

"One. He is no longer with us, and we miss him every day. How 'bout you?"

Ginny called our shared disdain a refusal to "talk about the curtains." Suddenly the way we had interacted with friends and acquaintances for our entire lives no longer seemed sufficient. Everyone seemed petty, even obnoxious, but I knew it was me who had changed, and there was no road leading back to the ghost of my former self. I often attempted to decipher whether this new me was good or bad. But I soon left this debate behind, accepting that it was as worthless as a curtain conversation. It was just me, the one without Eliot.

Marital strife, awkward conversations, and canine finger-pointing served as an introduction to what has now become my unshakeable shadow known as grief. I had landed precisely where I had spent a lifetime steering away from, and now that I was here, I was certain of only one thing: there would be no pretending. I was not walking the party line. If it was a bad day, I told you. If I momentarily lost faith and wondered where God went, then I was not acting otherwise in order to make others more comfortable. I was not comfortable with my reality and did not see why others needed me to fluff their pillows either.

Ginny and I were undecided with what to do about the blog. We discussed being done with it, and then I would find myself pushing "submit" on a new post detailing how we were approaching Christmas without Eliot or the latest idea on what we would do with our lives with him gone.

Scrambled in sadness, I masked the reason for keeping up the blog in a hero's cape, telling myself that I would put my grief on exhibit in hopes that it might help someone else with theirs. But I knew better, the truth nagging all along. It was me who needed the process of distilling all the rage and confusion into a tangible sentence. Typically I failed at this goal, knowing my words did not quite grasp the complexities or represent us accurately, but upon that rarest of occasions when a sentence pinpointed true north, it was exhilarating.

Writing through the journey forced me to acknowledge the presence of characters other than the obvious albatross of emotion. Loss leaves those left here not blinded but with tunnel vision—unable to imagine anything peripheral of the pain. Without making time for reflection, the cantankerous showstopper of absence always stayed center stage on the unseen production of my mind and heart. But stillness was the gift that allowed me to look stage-left, where the understudies were hanging out, taking breaks in the shadows. Truth, hope, and perspective came into view slowly, by faith, and never easily. Writing was the schoolteacher constantly slapping my wrist with a ruler and forcing me into a posture of silence, a discipline I otherwise opposed regardless of my awareness of the need for it.

There were two months remaining before a spring semester return to law school, and I was able to realize a small, unspoken aspiration of mine—moving to first-name status at the local coffee shop. I would order something other than coffee at the counter, find a booth, and settle in for an indeterminable amount of time.

Thus, I stumbled into a healthy grieving situation rather than aiming for it. With the coincidental gift of time, what I did was all that I could, which turned out to be just what I needed. I sat and read. I wrote and cried—big awkward tears accompanied by loud sniffing, forcing the coffee crowd to pretend as if they did not notice. I prayed with head in hands, drinking chai tea lattes that I couldn't afford with long sips, being sure to savor the few places I still found enjoyment.

I avoided all books on grief and loss, though many were given and suggested. I headed straightway down a path I could never advise to another—feeling strongly as though I wanted to experience the road ahead for myself. I felt no need to possess the ability to label my current status as "stage three of five" or be able to name my foes when I met them. I figured if I were being forced down the very road that I sought to avoid, I would eventually arrive without the use of a map.

Eliot had left us both empty and full—empty with aching arms to hold him and voluminous rooms of hopes unmet, but full with lessons gleaned from his days and a newfound clarity that colored life in such a way that I can scarcely recall what I was like before I was the way I am now.

In ninety-nine days, truths underpinning all of life had moved from my head into my veins, and when such is the case, one must find an outlet—some way to construct a new world that acknowledges the drumbeat that suddenly renders all else mute. Eliot's life and leaving had changed me. Prayers, tea, and writing were precious tools that helped me discover how.

Though I was waiting for a crisis of faith, none came. I had seen and heard of countless others walking away from God when life exploded, so I expected I would at least battle doing the same.

However, for me it was not like that. Eliot's life served only to bolster my pre-existing belief that there was a God who was real and alive. But He was not precisely who I had thought. Instead of a crisis, I got a mystery. That devious little fellow I called "God" had wriggled out of his cage and refused to go back inside.

So I wrote for me—and for Ginny too. I read each post aloud to her, asking if it truly conveyed the way we felt, and then doubled back to correct the few places she wasn't sure of. It was therapeutic to agree that *someone* knew how we felt, even if it was us.

Though I did make quite a few people uncomfortable along the way with my open approach to my path of pain, I also found others—a ragtag bundle of compatriots—relieved to find they were not alone in their ongoing battles between hope and hurt. I learned to call pain *pain*—and joy *joy*—abandoning a learned practice of insisting my faith necessitates that all is always fine. I admittedly felt the pull to comply by pasting false smiley faces on endings where none belonged. Even though, for some deviant reason, I do enjoy making people squirm, the driving force of my relentless pursuit of honestly dealing with the pain of losing Eliot came from something far greater. I know that anything less than the truth reflects my belief that my true self is unworthy of His love and is thereby an admission that His grace must fall short.

But an honest pursuit of Him throughout all of it was all that He asked, and it was enough. It is in my weakness that He is strong. With my doubts He fashioned faith. With my anger He crafted patience. With my longings He reminded me of His promises. God is glorified most when I am honest with Him, myself, and those around me. His faithfulness is shown in the things He has brought forth from my loss. He was not who I thought, not as I hoped. Through stillness before Him in my darkest of moments, He was beckoning me to come closer to Him, not as I wished Him to be, but as He is.

Eleven
BIG HAIR, BIG SMILES, AND BIG LIES

We never paid for cable in our first five years of marriage, although we did have it for a brief season in Fort Worth. It was a magical time, those weeks in Texas with free cable. Although I saw public service announcements deriding my apparent crime of serendipitously gleaning channels from the coax ferry, I somehow still managed to sleep at night—but only after an hour or so of television.

I would love to chalk up our cable forbearance to something such as morals or an attempt to embolden creative juices; instead, it was solely a decision based on an attribute of mine I choose to call *thrifty*. I despise committing to future payments for anything and avoid licking stamps to send monthly checks as though it had been proven that stamp glue exposure causes cancer—just one of the many ways I trick myself into saving funds.

When we brought Eliot home from the NICU, it was decided that we would join the rest of the modern world and actually pay monthly rates to have an assortment of channels piped into our living room. I overcame the imaginary hazard to my health only by way of the justification that our home was now the place we would all reside for large portions of every day. The coincidental alignment of football season did not hurt either.

In actuality, the television was rarely on during those months with Eliot. If it was, it served as the backdrop to our true focus. The main exceptions were those early-morning hours when he was fast asleep on the couch. I would flip through to find a documentary on any given subject or VH1—anything to keep me company, particularly on those nights that followed the more difficult days. These were the lonely nights, watching music videos at full volume to help me stay awake between intermittent pleas and prayers for a good day tomorrow.

In the days after Eliot there was a plethora of time to watch television. In doing so, I noticed a trend that had managed to evade my radar, most likely due to a half decade's fasting from the magic box. There were preacher types on the tube—lots of them. And not only that, but entire channels were dedicated to pastors, preachers, deacons, and brothers—all reading from the same script, one that was strangely unfamiliar to my well-churched ears.

This was a serious case of unfortunate timing. I sat frozen, the remote aimed and ready to continue the search for Dog the Bounty

Hunter, yet inexplicably unable to look away. Although the messenger changed, the pasted-on smiles and promises spoken in tones of absolute certainty never did. Through all of the twisted Bible stories and flashing phone numbers to call with prayer requests or monetary gifts, my heart distilled the message in an instant: if I had only believed enough, then God would have healed him.

This oft-repeated spiel is commonly referred to as the *prosperity gospel*. According to these folks, God wanted to pour out His "blessing" on me—if only I could muster up enough of something.

Still holding the remote and feeling nauseated, I wondered if this message might have appealed to me had I stumbled on it just before my life forked and headed straightway in a different direction than these gospel thieves proclaimed. For I was led unwillingly toward true blessing and found prosperity cloaked in weakness, available to all who would kneel low for viewing.

For God was there for me, despite me. His love did not wane when my faith weakened. He was sufficient, a truth displayed most brilliantly in the blinding light of my own insufficiency. When I cannot pray harder, when I am unable to conjure up more belief within my own bones, He never leaves. His God-ness and His good-ness do not rely or require of me what I cannot do without Him. If I had a scintilla of hope, it was sourced in Him and not of my own will.

The prosperity pundits want a transaction. They have fashioned a god to meet their own needs on their own terms, and they market their vile heresy to the desperate—tickling the ears of the hurting and the needy. This god is a response to the priorities of this world; but another beckons us instead to a kingdom altogether upside-down to this ragged world, a place so unlike this realm that what we thought were our desires are shown to be only a shallow inkling of the depths reserved for His beloved in a land beyond this one. The gospel counters a formulaic slot-machine genie with a God who wants your heart. He seeks a relationship. He wants you to know His love—one that overcomes all circumstances and overwhelms every hurt that this fallen world can bring your way. He is the blessing. He is enough.

He is not looking for you to will more faith or give more money or try harder in your own strength—though one sliver of Him and you will do all this and more. He is asking you to die, to trust Him in spite of this world, to know that He has overcome and that He alone is where your troubled heart finds rest.

Though the fig tree should not blossom, nor fruit be on the vines, the produce of the olive fail and the fields yield no food, the flock be cut off from the fold and there be no herd in the stalls, yet I will rejoice in the LORD; I will take joy in the God of my salvation. God, the LORD, is my strength; he makes my feet like the deer's; he makes me tread on my high places (*Habakkuk 3:17-19*, ESV).

GET BETTER ALREADY

Though the easiest foes were found on television, believers in general seemed to struggle with my process of grief, their default settings apparently baffled. Outside of those close friends in whom we sought shelter were the fringe folks who offered comments and insights revealing their own versions of where I stood. I believed in their God but openly aired my grievances and would not allow them to walk away unscathed if they attempted to place a bow or bumper sticker on my pain.

"Well, let's be thankful for what we did get."

"It's all about His glory."

"It's all working out for good."

It seemed that some approached me as an opportunity to quote their favorite go-to verse for just such a situation as this one. They seemed perfectly happy with themselves, a kid walking away from the chalkboard after correctly solving the problem posed by the teacher. But I was left wondering how the fact that God was in control did not serve to turn me against Him.

For the first time, I began asking the Lord not to let me hate those who called themselves by His name. For reasons beyond me, the followers of a faith built squarely on the graphic death of a man named Jesus, seemed now most uncomfortable with death itself. They sang choruses about the Cross and the blood while begging me not to focus on loss.

It seemed their unstated goal was to get me back to my old self, the one before Eliot—moving me off the conveyor belt of loss and into a place where I only smiled, never questioned, and eventually graduated from sadness, to a place where I brought fellow grievers casserole and counsel to follow my lead: *buck up, speak only in clichés, and don't forget to show those teeth.*

For the most part, the reason I wanted to punch these folks had nothing to do with the content of useless reaches into their grab bag labeled "Things to say when this or that happens." Rather, it was the attitude that linked Jesus with a painless life, pulling out their scratchpads and prescribing Jesus pills to dull the pain and fix it by the morning.

Scripture revealed a very different picture of processing pain and loss—one these quick-fix medics quoted only in pieces, much like a certain serpent in a famous garden. Believers did not grieve as those with no hope, but *did* grieve nonetheless for a world off-kilter and tragically flawed.

The eleventh chapter of John presents an interesting story for those made uncomfortable by my experience of grief. Jesus gets word from Mary and Martha that their brother, Lazarus, has become ill. He then states the following upon receiving the news:

This illness does not lead to death. It is for the glory of God, so that the Son of God may be glorified through it (*John 11:4*, ESV).

Jesus opts to remain a couple more days before turning His attention toward Lazarus. Upon arrival, He is welcomed with a no-confidence vote of "too little too late." While Jesus meandered, Lazarus had succumbed, and his lifeless body lay in the tomb where it had been for the last four days. Mary and Martha lament the prolonged absence that could have saved their brother while Jesus exhibits no regard for time nor their notions of what is already in the past.

Allow me to jump ahead and hand out the spoiler. Jesus is going to ask onlookers to remove the stone that covers the tomb, and with just three words He is going to restore life to His friend. Lazarus will live again.

But I have skipped a certain part of the story in my re-telling—a part that I did not notice until I experienced grief myself. Once I had, what before had gone unnoticed became my fixation within the whole story—a shimmering light that overwhelmed the entire narrative in days after losing Eliot.

When Jesus saw her weeping, and the Jews who had come with her also weeping, he was deeply moved in his spirit and greatly troubled. And he said, "Where have you laid him?" They said to him, "Lord, come and see." Jesus wept (*John 11:33-35*, ESV).

What are you doing, Jesus? You are the very one who knows beyond a shadow of a doubt that this event—every detail—is all for the glory of the Father, the only one who is aware of the fact that within mere minutes Lazarus will be dead no more and that there will be no reason to despair.

It is within this framework that the Son of God grieves death. He weeps over loss and the hurt of others. He is deeply moved and troubled by the pain that death has introduced into the world. The overcomer of death pauses and acknowledges the pain and anguish that his losing foe has wrought.

It seemed that others were most uncomfortable with my own acknowledgment—as if somehow experiencing pain meant not believing that things will be set right in the end, a notion that somehow tears and grief give credit to the foe and do not acknowledge the One who will in the end always overcome.

And yet the reality of what will be does not negate the experience of pain today. Jesus wept in full knowledge that Lazarus would soon walk out of the tomb that held him. No glory was robbed. No falsehood was given credence. One cannot accurately celebrate victory over a foe he or she refuses to acknowledge. Those most hurt will be the loudest ones at the party trumpeting death's demise. Jesus wept, and I felt full freedom to join Him.

While there existed an overwhelming pull from onlookers just to move on, I heard another's whispered invitation to lean into the suffering—to slow down and place my pain under the microscope—to view losing my son as a window to understanding instead of something to endure and overcome.

Channel-surfing those smiling pastors, *blessing* was redefined in shades of gold and green. But I have known blessing, and I have grieved with a God who not only let me grieve but also became my companion. I did not find all the answers to the questions I posed. Instead, I found intimacy with the one I was asking. I know God more but understand Him less.

Twelve
HOLES IN THE FENCE

Ginny and I were now faced with a question that I cannot say ever actually surfaced but of which we were both intensely aware: *Would we have more children?*

Somewhere around the age of four and continuing for longer than I want to admit, I had a friend named Marty. There was nothing wrong with Marty; he came over to my house often to play, and unlike my dominant, older sister, he participated in whatever adventure I had cooked up for that particular day. Marty willingly manned the mast while I, ever the capable captain, barked orders of "Land ho!" while steering us to islands just beyond the red metal bunk bed that served as our vessel. When sea adventures ceased, we headed outside for some game with that day's ball of choice.

Marty was a good sport and smart enough; not once did he poke fun at the glasses that encompassed my face and served as the topic of conversation with so many of the other kids. He was my best friend, and had you asked, I would have readily told you that I loved him.

I eventually lost touch with Marty but fondly recall my introduction to friendship and even now catch myself juxtaposing my current best friends with all my former ones.

Ginny and I recently purchased our first home. Every last one of our friends had managed to clear this obstacle to adulthood long before us, but we were quite committed to the idea of renting and fairly pleased with our unpopular lack of ownership—only caving in as it become apparent that the sideways real estate market enabled us to purchase a home for less than we could rent the equivalent. Thus has been our reluctant introduction to home ownership, but we have come to love our little ranch home on Palmer—although I miss picking up the phone when the roof leaks rather than picking up the bill, far more than you can imagine.

Finding a home that we both liked and could actually afford proved somewhat akin to the difficulty level more often associated with the likes of nuclear fusion. I am a cruel paradox when it comes to tastes and preference: I have strong opinions—always a little more on the fray than in the mainstream, but my budget is as tight as a Botoxed brow. Therefore, with big-ticket items such as a home, there is almost never overlap in what I like and what I will pay for. Thus, I do not have what I actually want and can be found secretly coveting the purchases of my friends while peppering them with questions as to how they could ever justify paying so much. I have just enough taste to know I am wearing, carrying, or living in something I would rather not. I have often wished for the lack of taste I see evidenced all around by seemingly happy people. Fewer predilections seem the only hope for overcoming my conflicted situation, because I cannot imagine my pain at handing over funds will abate.

Somehow, though, the house on Palmer won us both over. We like to refer to the two-bedroom, one-bath house built in 1952 as "mid-century modern"—admittedly a little more *mid-century* than *modern*. The exterior is a mixture of rock and wood. There is a single-car garage, so narrow I cannot imagine a car actually fitting inside, which is perfectly fine with us as Ginny confiscated this space long ago as a hideout to sketch and create various jewelry designs.

Recently discussions pertaining to the house have centered on the security of our red-and-rock home. I have had to travel a bit as of late, often leaving Ginny alone for short stretches of time. She gets along well enough, sleeping less but reading more, inviting friends over on nights that seem eerie.

The Palmer house is situated near a college campus in Fayetteville, right on the cusp of where apartments and temporary housing meet older, established neighborhoods. The local mosque is just two blocks away, and the football stadium nearly shades our home when the sun glints at just the right angle. There are hills and a tiny park; it is quaint and unspectacular with no McMansions for miles.

While my propensity to avoid commitment will not allow me to use "never," suffice it to say that the suburbs, while not evil, are not a welcomed prospect for either of us. These are just a few of the characteristics comprising some of the main draws of Palmer for us—within blocks of our home there walks all rank-and-file whether by age, color, religion, or income.

By way of security, we have a motion light that, on the rare occasion there is movement present, illuminates the left portion of the house. There is no security system, although we do have a chain-link fence in the backyard. It contains Wilson—but this dog of ours is infinitely more prone to lick someone than protect anyone. Thus, when leaving, bags in hand and car started, I always attempt to estimate and manage Ginny's level of fear—enough to lock the doors but not so much as not to sleep. Of course, she needs none of this, but the ritual makes me feel manly, so she obliges.

There is a truth that many labor to ignore as a way of fending off evil. No matter our effort, the truth remains. We are not safe. And although reason dictates wearing helmets and locking doors, that same reason—when further applied to the world we find ourselves in—reveals that there is no escape from vulnerability.

As much as I can, I will remove those things that threaten to cause me harm. But at the end of the day I must also acknowledge that my efforts cannot hold back all the things I wish they could. Eliot taught us a thing or two about control. All facades were exposed as lacking, and both of us were left facing the fact that we were helpless and pathetic at precisely the time it seemed we were most needed.

We would try to have more children.

Although letting go of control is awful, pretending to be in control of that which we are not is even worse. Besides, it is only through the holes in the fence that the beauty enters in, along with the pain. Our structures of protection serve to keep out blessing as well. All is intertwined and wound up together, pain and beauty, and both advance only as the fences fall and the gate swings open.

We began to pray that God would give us as much joy in future children as we had found with Eliot. We knew, left to ourselves, we would build fences around our hearts in order to avoid the pain we now knew; but in our best moments, we leave the gate wide open, exposed and ready for love to enter again.

My friend Marty died around age seven. It wasn't as bad as it seems—because he lived only in my imagination. I had made him up, a by-product of creativity and boredom. But I was serious when I said I loved him. I did. There came an age when I killed him off in exchange for real friends, ones who wanted to play games that I did not and laughed at my "ship" and my glasses.

But at some point in growing up, I decided I preferred a world with complexity and pain over a safe friend who always let me win but did not actually exist.

Thirteen
BLOOMS

I quit blogging. The process of weekly writing had meandered from therapeutic to chore status, and I racked my brain for new content, but the reality was that I did not feel like writing about where we now found ourselves. We could not get pregnant.

I left this tidbit out of public consumption for fear that people would feel sorrier for us than they already did. We did not need that. A beautiful video telling of Eliot's life had managed to fool some folks into thinking we were some sort of mythic beings, but I found myself constantly reminding people I had never met that it was just six minutes, and if they wanted to follow me around or ask my friends, they would soon find that I was nothing special.

We got pregnant with Eliot upon just the thought that maybe it was time for two to become three. But now we were thinking and trying and calculating, and nothing was happening. For months after Eliot, we knew there existed a window of time when we were not ready for another child. Although we missed parenting so much that it physically hurt, it was obvious to us in days after Eliot that we were not at a place to welcome another. As time passed and we learned how to make loss a part of our lives, we began thinking that maybe, just maybe, we were now ready for our second child. It seemed someone disagreed.

The doctors and geneticists all concurred there was nothing we should do differently. Trisomies were not genetically passed on but were instead a spontaneous occurrence that could happen again, but the chances were infinitesimal. Of course, this did little to assuage the shouting voices in our heads telling them that once you have lived the long odds, statistics no longer hold the comfort they once did.

As our doctors attempted to assist with our struggle to get pregnant, they somehow managed to move intimacy from spontaneous, romantic frolic to dated-tallies on a spreadsheet. And in a sentence the eighteen-year-old version of me could not fathom, baby-making was moving into the category of sorting the recyclables. But we minded every last instruction, afraid the slightest alteration would ensure another month of negative results on the pregnancy tests.

Watching Ginny's eyes drop with what seemed like our monthly failure was beginning to make me angry.

Was it not enough yet?

Is it too much to ask?

Are you just being cruel?

I felt as if we should now be exempt—or better yet, that God owed us something. We had walked down the painful path, and now every path from here forward should be lined with rose petals. It was God's job to see that I was finished with heartache. Go on and teach the next person the lessons Pain holds, 'cause I got them and can revisit those notes without experiencing it all again. I blame this attitude on Job. Whenever the worst subsides, I expect everything that was lost to be returned—and then some. But our house was empty and our prayers were weakened. We wanted more children. Days passed with ovulation kits and pregnancy tests; days became months; months became seasons.

Though the childbearing front was a consistent source of sadness, hope was creeping like an ivy—moving leaf by leaf in its unnoticed but persistent way. Ginny's smile had returned, maybe not as often but more brilliant than ever. I was becoming thankful for the hard-earned eyes that I now viewed the world through. My return to law school had bolstered the notion that my son had allowed me to become a different person when I sat again in the desk where I had sat with such different posture only months before. I could not pretend nor convince myself that finals, internships, and bar exams were of dire importance.

Where I wanted a return in terms of children, there was first a work to be done within. The yield came in quiet moments of reflection on how I had been changed by the life of my son. I had come nearer to the heart of God, seeing the world and all its trappings with a clarity I had never known before. Although I wanted to rush headlong into the next hollow promise of diversion—new babies, new career, anything—instead, I was called into a season of waiting. The propensity for one to remain occupied after a difficult season is a predictable one. My attempts to self-rebound were thwarted by our inability to conceive, and I was forced to pull up a chair and sit around the table with my struggles, emotions, and lessons. Having much to say from this silent period with these companions, I returned to the blog, nine months after my last post and a year and a half after Eliot's passing.

FRIDAY, APRIL 11

We're still here.

Posted by Matt Mooney at 10:34 a.m.   196 comments

Hello, all. We wanted to drop an update into the blogosphere.

We have been overwhelmed by the amount of e-mail and encouragement that have continued in our absence. Thanks to all who have made the effort to let us know that you care.

In the way of update, Ginny and I are at work in much the same way as we left. Ginny's pursuits in the jewelry business continue, and she is hoping to take her ideas to another level soon with the unveiling of a new direction. I am in my last semester of law school with a few more hours this semester than I would recommend, but the powers that be have promised to let me out upon attaining this magic number of credits. Thus, the schedule reads as follows: finish school, graduation, and then bar exam.

And yes, I am still not thinking I will actually practice law. We'll see—I'm open. Even still, I threaten to walk away from school, but this stems mainly from the awkward laughter and concern that this remark conjures up in my wife and friends. What a good woman!

One of the greatest joys has been the realization of a nonprofit idea that we had hoped to start. The name of the nonprofit is "99 Balloons." The first activity we have pursued is a respite night for special-needs families to drop off their children with special needs along with the siblings. Thus, some parents have been able to receive a long-overdue night off. The name of the night is "rEcess."

rEcess has provided many highlights, but at the top has been the opportunity to watch others jump in and serve with humility and grace. I can now say that I know a place where Christ is on display each month, and we are humbled to be a part of it. It has become increasingly obvious that the whole thing has nothing to do with Ginny and me; rather, it is much bigger than that.

The website is still under development, but feel free to check it out: www.99balloons.org.

And now we segue into what I will call a letter—I believe in restoration. Not too long ago Fayetteville got our big snow of the year. We pretty-much get one a winter to justify the sled in the garage. Previous to what we'll affectionately call the "winter storm," I was talking to a friend on the phone who had become aware of the forecasted six inches.

Aside: We got less than three inches of snow, which was gone by brunch, but you must understand that it was our weatherman's annual shot at being a big-timer—with the exception of delivering the news that a wall cloud might have been spotted near Goshen by Hal, one of the station's weather-watchers. I digress.

I believe in restoration.

On this phone call, my friend was lamenting the future of his almost-budded flowers and how again this year's beauty would be stopped before it began. Now to my parent's chagrin, I have never been accused of having a green thumb, and even the manly yearn to mow is foreign to me. So admittedly, flower-worry was not on my radar when talk of a blizzard began.

Within a week of the whiteout, I had another encounter with lawns and gardens. I am a creature of habit and pretty-much walk Wilson (the dog) on the same route daily. It is upon this route where I take stock of the neighborhood and busy myself trying to ensure that the dog's business does not occur in the lawns of neighbors I actually like. Certain aspects along this urban trail do not go unnoticed: my neighbor still does not know that the trash can is supposed to stay curbside only one day a week. Yet another has not received word that his yard is actually not a junk museum.

It's not all bad on the dog walk. Not having a green thumb does not mean I cannot be green with envy when I see a great yard.

You know the one—plush, green, thick, the one we all spy on to confirm our suspicion that the work is hired labor. It somehow makes us feel better if it is.

In our neck of the woods it lies just two blocks away and is referred to only as "the yard." I always take stock of this lot and ruminate about how pathetic it is to care so much about grass. (It's my problem—I'm working on it.) On a recent walk while deriding the pitiful owner in the secrecy of my mind, I realized that the yard looked terrible. It was dusk, so I gleefully moved closer to examine what had occurred.

Sure enough, the yard was not plush. In fact, it was dead. The secret was out. The lot had been purposely burned down to nothing but charred, black earth.

And that is what Ginny and I have been doing—learning from life that although all that's good can be covered over to the point where no bloom is forthcoming, and all that's for viewing is dead earth where vitality once resided, herein lies a strange but beautiful recipe for life: plush, full life.

I have long examined and not concluded why sometimes blooms come back more beautiful than ever, while other blossoms never return. And I can only point to the One who willingly died that life could take root in me.

I believe in restoration.

P.S. We're pregnant.

Fourteen
MYTH

In this world you will have trouble.
—Jesus, John 16:33

The airport is always my reminder of the
lengths to which we all go to in order to make
ourselves feel secure. I get it. I even prefer
it—long lines, shoes off, baggage X-rays, and
liquid containers no bigger than three ounces. We now debate technology that produces
images of our naked bodies but can also better sense materials for blowing stuff up.

Regardless of which side you find yourself in this debate, we can all agree that it is a discussion that only years ago would have been outrageous—before men boarded four planes and ravaged entire cities in acts of cowardice that played out on television sets everywhere.

Our culture hungers for control, and when we cannot control, we build facades to convince ourselves otherwise. I have a soapbox when it comes to terrorists that goes like this: "Stop acting like these thugs did some feat of genius. It is not hard to destroy or kill or maim. If that is your end goal, it is unfortunately both low and attainable."

But I think our culture does not want to admit that. We do not want to admit that someone dead-set on destruction can achieve those ends in spectacular fashion with the intellect of a ten-year-old—because then we are left facing the reality that many of us construct our lives to *avoid*.

It is out of my hands.

THE NINETY-NINE PERCENT

Ginny typed the following after Eliot's passing. My mind envisions her intermittently propping both arms on her rounded belly—seven months pregnant with our second. Rising up among her words, I see a theme hanging in midair, suspended over the page.

We are not safe.

Though a baby was coming and we had been reassured countless times by multiple medical professionals that nothing was wrong this time around, she turned the bullhorn backward, reminding us that our hope cannot lie in safety but solely in the One who assures that His presence is sufficient.

FRIDAY, AUGUST 29

The Safe Myth

Posted by Ginny Mooney at 11:30 a.m.   20 comments

My in-laws are wonderful people. Not long ago the family went out to a local Mexican spot to grab some dinner. The whole group was there: my husband, his parents, his sister, and her two little girls. As is routine in restaurants, we were seated, and the waiter took our drink order and then made his way back to take the meal order. Then, as is routine with my in-laws, my mother-in-law pulls her purse into her lap and begins to search for it. My father-in-law is looking in anxious anticipation of it. It is of vital importance to their dining experience, and I have never seen them eat out without it. Then she finds it and sets it as a centerpiece on the table: the travel-size bottle of anti-bacterial hand gel, claiming to kill up to ninety-nine-point-nine-percent of germs. She coats herself with it, then he coats himself with it, and they attempt to get everyone at the table to coat themselves with it. There truly is nothing like the aromas of alcohol and sizzling fajitas colliding.

I politely decline. I can only speculate as to how the restaurant gel routine came about. Maybe my father-in-law saw a very convincing commercial, or possibly my mother-in-law had a friend tell her of the preventative powers of the gel. Regardless of how they got there, they have their gel. I guess we all have our gel, something that makes us feel better about the inevitable "germs" that are out there in the world. I would venture to say that for most, the deep-rooted issue of the gel is one of fear intermingled with control. We fear something, something we don't like or would be unpleasant for us, and that fear leads us to think we have to control the situation to make it right or clean or safe or healthy or better. It's sort of like when we learned about *if-then* clauses in grade school.

If I use this hand gel, *then* I will not eat germs.

If I have a net on a trampoline, *then* I can bounce and not get hurt.

If I eat right and exercise, *then* I will not get cancer.

If I study and search enough, *then* I will have it all figured out.

I have no problem with any of those things. They are wonderful things. Safety nets, hand gels, healthy lifestyle, and knowledge all speak of responsibility and stewardship, both of which I am a huge fan and both of which honor God. My issue is not with the *if* but with the *then.*

We have this tendency in our comfortable Western culture to hang our hats on those *thens*. Everyone feels above them, the harm, hurt, accidents, pain, sickness, death that's a natural part of our mortal lives and the fallen world in which we live. We feel above it all, because when the fear of those things creeps in, we go into super-control mode. More hand gel. Taller nets. A newer vitamin. Harder helmets. *I can control this fear! I can make my world safe!*

The truth is that the Creator of us, of the universe, of all that we are and see and experience is the only one in control. He is the only one who redeemed what went wrong in the garden on the Cross. He is the only one who sees past the momentary lack of safety and the hurt to the character being built in us in adversity. Not us—we cannot make all things right or safe and believe a lie when we think we can. Only one can—and does. I am no expert on the matter, and in fact, more times than I prefer I give into that sneaky lie. For instance, this *if-then* statement was floating around in my mind as Matt and I thought about starting a family. If I do everything right while I'm pregnant, then I will have a healthy baby.

A few months later, I was pregnant, and I did everything right. I drank no caffeine. I didn't drink alcohol. I didn't smoke or get near anyone who did. I took a prenatal vitamin every day. I exercised just enough, not too much and not too little. I drank a ton of water. I ate foods rich in vitamins and folic acid and DHAs and steered away from fast food. My showers were never too hot. I never lifted anything remotely heavy. I got plenty of rest, never lying on my back. I made sure not to stand for too long or sit for too long. Yep, I went through every *if* you could think of or read about. Still, God himself held in His hand my *then*. My *then* was not a healthy baby. My *then* was a sweet, beautiful, amazing, sick baby boy who lived for ninety-nine days. Thinking we can do enough to be safe and do enough for our kids to keep them safe is simply a myth. Only one holds our days in His hands.

> For you have delivered me from death and my feet from stumbling, that I may walk before God in the light of life (*Psalm 56:13*).

Hazel Emerson Mooney entered our world with loud lungs, instantly making her presence known to all within blocks of the hospital room—steps from where her brother was delivered. Her knack for leaving an impression has not yet abated. She is something else—a force to be reckoned with; a blond-headed, ballet twirling, Adele-lip-syncing force of nature. And I am the father my son made me to be. I let more things go than I thought I would before I had a son, before I had a daughter. I laugh when she colors the walls with big, broad pen strokes—the ones we had just painted. I make sure the painter knows not to cover over her work when he returns for touch-ups.

Hazel did not care to sleep for the first eight months of her life. We tried it all—even trading messages with a self-described *sleep nanny* who acknowledged that Hazel was "one of a kind." We strangely derived much solace from Hazel's ability to break someone other than us. But she sleeps now, and we have even begun using the word *sweet* when describing her—an adjective we evaded in the early stages, steering more toward descriptions that avoided her demeanor. She was *beautiful, fabulous,* and *strong-willed.*

However, once the gift of words came into her world, it seemed we may have pigeonholed her a little early. Between the first tooth and wobbly step, she gained a spirit to match those looks. And just about the time we were settling in to a life with the sweet version of Hazel, Ginny was pregnant again.

I should in no way be surprised upon this revelation, seeing as I was actively involved in the process and do have a sufficient grasp on the mechanics of it all, but I was. Getting pregnant with Hazel had taken such effort and time, along with some extra help from the medical community. But this time around, it took little more than locking eyes. We rolled with it—laughing at the suddenly bountiful crop where barren land stood mere months before.

Ginny, who had been a perfect picker thus far, made no guess at the gender of this one. I committed to a girl, reasoning that I was totally the kind of guy who would be fine with all girls since I harbored scant desire to wake up a mini-me, deck out in camouflage, and go looking to shoot the first thing that moved. Besides, I had my son.

Anderson Abel Mooney left me zero for three. We call him *And-ers*, not *On-ders*. He has Ginny curls on his head and enough energy to power the grid of a medium-sized city. He throws everything and has a justice bent that makes sure everyone is always included—whether he or she wants to be or not. Ginny and I settled into life with the twosome known only as "the rascals." If the fact that they were born fifteen months apart does not convey quite a bit to you already, then you obviously have no children of your own. Yet throughout all the chaos, on the better days nothing can suppress the absolute joy we derive from the moments now beheld as *holy* in the day-to-day caring for our children. We are living our dream.

We are a family of five. Hazel said "e-yatt" for Eliot soon after her first word, and Anders knows he has a brother. Ginny and I often lament the fact that our children were born into our grief, and we all will bear up under the burden brought by loss together. But we would have it no other way. Anything else would be pretending. Instead, we have welcomed these little lives into our own as they truly are—tragically beautiful.

NO SUFFICIENT BALM

We are almost living our dream. As we began to tell people that we were pregnant after Eliot, there seemed a communal, monolithic sigh of relief from those we encountered. I fully understand this, and I undoubtedly joined in with the chorus adding my own thankful exhale. But therein slithers another swarthy salesman peddling bottles to cure whatever may ail. We who grieve, as well as those around us, are weak prey for illusions—always prone to seek out a quick escape from a reality we do not want to face. More children did not make it all better; Ginny and I unearthed this unwanted treasure before either one came. Any notion otherwise would saddle our children with doing what we ourselves could not. No matter the effort expended in searching, I have found no quick fix for the loss of my son. Sad people make the worst kind of suckers—prone to take the bait on any offer claiming to take the pain away or even allow us to neglect the pain but for a moment.

In fact, Hazel and Anders have brought vivid colors of joy onto our landscape as well as ushered in new phases of grief with every accomplishment attained that their brother did not.

How do we celebrate Hazel's one-hundredth day without tears? Her first steps? Anders's first day at school? Sports? Friends? Proms?

We are just beginning to see what it is we have lost.

A part of us is missing, even as the whole enlarges. We miss him every day. He cannot be "brought up" by way of conversation, having never wandered to the background. If someone were to sit outside our home peering in, they would find a home filled with toddler fights and toddler fun, but their eyes could not be trusted to interpret the whole. And this is precisely the truth that we cling to with a white-knuckled grip of desperation. Our entire story—as well as our lone hope—is bound together in a reality obscured by this world. What the eye beholds is not all that exists.

Fifteen
INSTEAD

I now see that the pursuit of safety is a creepy vine that begins small and well-intentioned but soon takes over, choking out life as it climbs its subject. In the wake of losing Eliot, I began scouring for what good God is. If I did not get the answer to my prayers and was not exempt from the deep pangs of loss, then what could God be held accountable for? If He did not do what I wanted, then what—if anything—*was* He doing?

In admittedly pathetic style, I was looking for the guarantees that came with the product known as *God*. I began seeing that I and many of those around me had unwittingly forged a view of God influenced by the culture of consumerism in which we are immersed.

I wanted God to be The Gap. Provide me with what I think I need—a khakis sort of life—and I'll be a faithful, card-carrying customer. But He did not oblige. He did not give me what I asked for. And I hated the product that was supplied in place of what I sought. Where I wanted slacks, he handed me rags. And I began to see quite clearly that God makes a horrible store manager.

If I could not count on God to save my son—the most monumental request I had ever brought before Him—then what could I count on Him for? In those quiet days of grief and mourning after Eliot, I felt as though God, ever patient with my misperceptions of Him, was calling me in voiceless manner to a pursuit far greater than mere happiness and onto a path that was anything but safe.

He alone was to be the object of my pursuit—not the illusion of safety, but Him. Nothing else—just Jesus. The guarantees accompanying such a pursuit were not as I had hoped:

All that He is—is enough.

He will never leave.

He is at work now and in the days to come.

ALL THAT HE IS—IS ENOUGH

I am sure I have opined on something akin to this notion many times—even dishing it out to others in heaping portions when I sensed their discontent or complaining.

Here you go—a steaming cup of "He is enough" should cure what ails you.

Though I certainly had served it up before Eliot, I had not partaken for myself. The very thing I desired in greater portion than all I had known before—life for my son—was taken from me. I was met with a crisis: were the words on my lips of His sufficiency rooted in my heart or in my upbringing?

In the days of caring for Eliot—living in light of the weighty fears of his passing into eternity at any moment—and in the darkest of days after saying good-bye . . .

Today, when I awake and look into the eyes of my children, knowing I am not guaranteed another morning's gaze into their beloved faces . . .

In all my days—either He is enough, or that which I look to is not God. In Him alone my soul finds rest, and all my desires are met in Him—the very desires I am so quick to exchange for the illusion of safety instead.

God said to Moses, "I am who I am" (*Exodus 3:14*).

HE WILL NEVER LEAVE

In the days and months after Eliot, I remember the intense feeling that no one else on the face of the planet understood what I was going through. And in so many ways, this assumption is a correct one. I am always quick to point out that grief—and all of life—is a path unique to each of us. Even Ginny and I experience missing Eliot in different ways, at different times, and through different triggers.

I recently stumbled onto a story of an elderly couple in India who had committed suicide after the loss of their cat. The former me would have laughed this off and moved ahead with my reading—scouring for some score in some game. And I am not pretending that I did not laugh, but the laughter was coupled with a welling-up of feelings that I did not anticipate. I found myself unable to move on, just sitting there and mourning a bit for this couple in a far-off land who lost Felix or Cupcake or whatever strange name the cat had—likely one with lots of Indian syllables I can't pronounce.

I don't know how the loss of a cat starts one down the road that leads to hopelessness. Though I am unsure of how *that* gets one *there*, I do know the route. I have visited *there*, trod the worn path of *there*, and can feel nothing but compassion for all who step foot on it. It is a road with signposts proclaiming that no one understands, that no one has been here before, and worse of all, that *I am alone*. But there is One who pulled me off this road before I even started down it; He did not thump me or preach or question how I could ever start down this path. He just showed up and offered to go down the road with me; and if He was with me, then I was not alone.

I am sure that neither death nor life, nor angels nor rulers, nor things present nor things to come, nor powers, nor height nor depth, nor anything else in all creation, will be able to separate us from the love of God in Christ Jesus our Lord (*Romans 8:38-39*, ESV).

Behold, I am with you always (*Matthew 28:20*, ESV).

HE IS AT WORK NOW AND IN THE DAYS TO COME

As a grieving believer, I find my hope for today is anchored within the reality that God is at work in and through the details of each hour and minute spent on this earth. He is with me, He is enough, and He is at work. With eyes cast upward, I have discovered that this daily expectation carries me forward. Not a day goes by that the hand of God is not busied with redemptive work within the troubles of this fleeting world.

Yet today yields only shadows of the completed work that is being accomplished. Ours is a hope that is realized in part within our days on this earth but ultimately anchored in a day to come. When the earth gives way, we call upon our faith that the earth and today are not all that exist. Redemption awaits us, and all will be set right in His coming kingdom.

When the perishable puts on the imperishable, and the mortal puts on immortality, then shall come to pass the saying that is written: "Death is swallowed up in victory. O death, where is your victory? O death, where is your sting?" (*1 Corinthians 15:54-55*, ESV).

FAITH FOR FRIDAYS

These were not the guarantees I sought. I wanted my way—my son—because honestly, I have a hard time seeing how He can do it any better than the way I would have. And when I can't muster within me the strength to hope in Him, I'm left crying out for a faith that is beyond my means.

As I tap out these very words on my outdated but faithful laptop, it is Good Friday, the very day on the Church's calendar set aside to mark and remember when Jesus was brutally beaten and killed. A fair question from an outsider to the Christian faith would be to inquire as to what is *good* about Good Friday? The question alone—one that I myself at times have had, but not had the gall to voice—reveals a bucket mentality believing in Good's and Bad's separate addresses, a life marked with avoiding Fridays and an inability to relent in an immersion of swirling colors of vivid pain and beauty.

Only by faith, and never by reason, do we stand in line for the very ride that all within us says to avoid. Jesus plunged headfirst into the swirl of the Cross—the one He prayed to avoid if at all possible. Scripture informs us that the lifeless body of Christ was laid in a tomb, where it remained for three days until He arose, overcoming death and ascending to heaven to reside with the Father on the day we commemorate as Easter Sunday. In my former bifurcated life, Easter is good, but Friday is not.

It seems that the Early Church fathers responsible for applying a moniker to this holy day must have grasped something that many believers struggle to comprehend—or possibly said better—something that today's believer never struggles with and therefore never understands. Paradox is counterintuitive, and taking hold of truths that contain elements of paradox requires a wrestling and reflection not embraced in a society intoxicated with the instantaneous.

Good Friday was horrible, and the Fridays in our own lives—the ones where we join Jesus in crying out to God, asking why He has forsaken us—must be acknowledged by us and by those around us as such. Good Friday was not good on *that* Friday. And only a trivial fool would have stood at the foot of the Cross and pointed out to Jesus that His resurrection was coming soon.

Good Friday is a statement of faith, a faith that believes, though all that the eye sees tells us we are defeated, exposed, and anything but safe. Without faith it is impossible to please God. Without God it is impossible to have faith. *Friday* is good only if our earthly eyes are wrong. We set our eyes on a hope that goes beyond this world. It is in this posture of faith that we get in line for the ride otherwise avoided. And those who choose to ride where others flee are rewarded with a new perspective that in one shallow breath names our own Fridays as both good and horrible.

The Cross reminds us that God's hope for us does not lie in temporary, status-quo safety. Instead, He asks us to trade in our most intimate desires for a life of faith—the kind of faith that does not allow for constructing safety nets, the kind of faith through which He is enough, and He is all we have.

Our security rests in knowing that He is with us, and seeking safety is only a detour on our heart's true desire to find rest in Him. A life lived spent building a self-made refuge is fatiguing, because one who does that can never rest in anything larger than himself or herself. And we all instinctively know we are insufficient. It is in letting go of the pursuit of safety that we find rest in the grasp of the One who is truly in control. By faith alone we believe that He is good, that He is with us, and that He is authoring a story of redemption and purpose that is not yet completed.

Today I need to go put training wheels on a bright pink princess bike—one I that I scavenged for Hazel from a friend's giveaway pile. She has outgrown her tricycle and patiently admired the hideously pink bike frame for far too long, waiting doggedly on her dad to fulfill his promise to attach two training wheels for assisted riding.

I will soon dutifully get out the toolbox and forage for the right screwdriver, being sure to attach each wheel with adequate torque to hold her weight, lest she fall—my attempt to keep Hazel from getting hurt. I will seek to fend off evil and heartache as well—with even greater fervor since Eliot—as I desire to keep her from the depths I have known. But even more so and with all intentionality I will point her to the One in whom something far greater than safety lies.

Not her daddy.

But her Father.

In this world you will have trouble. But take heart! I have overcome the world (*John 16:33*).

Sixteen
THE ART OF NOW

Do not worry about tomorrow, for tomorrow will worry about itself. Each day has enough trouble of its own.
—Matthew 6:34

Gene Weingarten wrote a masterful piece entitled "Pearls Before Breakfast" for the *Washington Post* outlining what can be deemed only as a social experiment. The idea was to plop this world's best attempt at beauty right into the middle of an overcrowded place on a typical day and see what happened. Just before 8 A.M. on Friday at L'enfant Plaza Station, one of the busiest Metro stops in Washington, D.C., a street musician pulled out a fiddle and played music for all present.

Only this youngish, white male was not just any street musician—he was Joshua Bell, a world-renowned violinist who often charges in excess of one hundred dollars per concert ticket. He is in the company of the few best classical musicians in the world. When he was four years of age his parents picked up on his potential as he strung rubber bands around dresser drawers, adjusting the drawers in order to vary the pitch of the bands.

He took his place at the station and began playing six of the finest pieces of music ever composed. Works by Bach and Schubert filled the air as strangers shuffled through the station in much the same manner as the day before. Bell decided he would play his own violin that day, an instrument handcrafted by Antonio Stradivari in the seventeen hundreds and carrying a price tag of more than three million dollars.

One of the greatest living musicians

Playing the world's best compositions

On an instrument reserved for masters

In the D.C. Metro Station during rush hour.

Weingarten outlines the discussions such an experiment spawned; scenarios were hypothesized regarding possible crowd reactions in order to avoid any mob scenes or disruptions to commuting. Over the span of forty-three minutes, beauty was on display—just past the countertops hawking porn and lotto tickets.

The experiment's outcome surprised all involved. There was never a crowd, as one thousand ninety-seven commuters hurried by without so much as a glance. Twenty-seven persons dropped money into Weingarten's violin case, totaling thirty-two dollars—for the man whose talents are often compensated at more than one thousand dollars a minute.

Bell could only describe the awkward feeling as being *ignored*, with the end of each piece seemingly unperceived. There were but precious few who stopped and took it in; the article details how the only demographic that displayed any attention in a consistent manner was young children, who were then, without fail, diverted by their parents or guardians.

Various experts were consulted and attempted to break down the realities and nuances of how something like this could happen. Explanations detailed the realities of context, the need for ideal viewing conditions, and modern-day busyness. On the whole, the day's activities could be described by the author as "art without a frame."

I was the one in a hurry to get somewhere, to do something. It was Eliot who halted my fast-stepping fall in line with the world. His life forced me to slow down, to drink deep of the making of a moment. I was unable to hold on to the beloved myth that there was ever more than the moment known as "now."

I am good at looking back; I can tell anyone who offers an ear, in detail, of that game I played in ninth grade and hit five three pointers in a row. I was on fire, and I remember. I can retell the precise moment I saw my bride walking the aisle toward me as I stood on the grounds of a Mississippi plantation home on that hot day, waiting and catching her eye, returning her smile. I enjoy casting a look back, ascribing meaning to moments that now reside over my shoulder.

I also like to look forward, or maybe I cannot help but do so. The worst mind-leaps are to days ahead and involve questions of having sufficient funds for the rascals' college tuition or an ample retirement to avoid dining on government cheese. But I have enjoyable imaginary looks forward as well.

My mind can spend hours contemplating an upcoming vacation—real or imagined. I look at my backyard and check through a list of things I will do when the time and money are available: hammock here, grill there, bigger deck stretching out an additional four feet with a portion screened in for all-weather use.

I envision Hazel walking down an aisle and my refusing to give her hand to any boy the likes of what I see walking the earth. I see her turning this heartbreak of my refusal at her wedding into a made-for-television movie when she becomes the first female astronaut to Mars.

I see me in in the bleachers of a game where Anders is playing something pertaining to a ball, and at the end of each game I'm telling him of the day I hit five three-pointers in a row.

But regarding the moment that is *now* is a different story altogether. It was Eliot who forced us into the paradigm where all we had was *now*. If we looked back or looked ahead, we would miss the opportunity of a memory that was waiting to be had. In addition, we knew there would be time to look back, and we both knew looking forward could be crushing, rendering us incapable of breathing in the moment before us, thereby robbing us of the moment's treasure. In this way, he merely brought clarity to what is true for me now, true for us all—yet a reality much easier to avoid with our own lives or the normal lives of those we love and orbit daily. In fact, though others may offer up my face as the poster boy for enjoying a moment, it is a lesson I lived with Eliot but struggle to implement today.

On my best days—the ones when I remember who I want to be and who I am—I slow it down the way Eliot taught me. I leave the memories for later. I turn down the noise of tomorrow—those things I cannot affect no matter the amount of time I spend mulling over them. I stop to see the beauty a day beholds. I take mental notes on the ways of my children and others around me; the young are the professional "moment-livers," having not yet filled their bags with sufficient memories to recount and not yet stained by the worries of tomorrow.

I look deep into the eyes of my daughter.

I acknowledge the stranger who is disrupting my plans.

I say yes when he asks me to play.

I turn off my phone with its endless accounts of lives other than my own.

I listen to my wife's every word.

I do not need to be told—as I swear I am by every grandparent who sees me with the rascals—to be sure to enjoy these days. They're right—but I already am. Our world is prone to choke out the now, keeping us too busy and too stressed with the cares of life. And we can be caught on a tic-tock swing, alternating between busyness and guilt for busyness.

I do not think it is by greater efforts alone that one can overcome the army of enemies conspiring to make a day too much to enjoy. Certainly Ginny and I did not possess the strength to partake in the moments that comprised Eliot's life in the face of the foreboding clouds of fear. When it is too much for us, we must call on something greater than ourselves. Each moment that we succeed in truly living in is a counterculture victory of massive proportion. It will not be your discipline that gets the acclaim when the credits roll. He tells us that He alone offers a peace that passes all understanding. This is the only way to catch the moments as they pass.

It is through the offer of His peace that we are awakened to the notes ringing out within the dinginess of a subway station. If we will be faithful to stop and ask, He will open our occupied ears to incomparable music all around us.

Seventeen

GOING TO GOD

In the absence of my son, I found myself often longing for this season of God's undeniable nearness in my pain. I now picture God going about His business carrying a ruler or some sort of heavy calculator. The greater the measure of my pain, the nearer He approached. In attempts to describe such a dance with the divine, I have referred to this season of my loss as the high-watermark point of my relationship with God. I have not drunk of His presence in this way for more than a moment, either before or since.

Sadly, I spent the greater portion of my life attempting to convince God to come near to me—that I was somehow good enough or possessed the faith that was sufficient—yet there He came when and where I least expected to see Him. He came with the hurt—entering with the ache and refusing to leave at my greatest time of need. Before I could not conjure Him up—now I could not escape Him.

Blessed are the poor in spirit, for theirs is the kingdom of heaven. Blessed are those who mourn, for they will be comforted (*Matthew 5:3-4*).

Pain was for me the frame surrounding God's beautiful work of art in this world—a kingdom brought into focus upon sorrow's entrance. What had escaped me now overwhelmed me: the beautiful work within the ashes. All along I had busied myself, shuffling by the street musician in search of one more skilled. I now find myself drawn to the lowlands. I seek out that which I spent my life avoiding before Eliot. It was pain that helped me see the symphony in the subway.

Where are the lame? I must make my home in their shadow. Where are the lowly—the ones despised? Where is pain at this moment? Because I have tired of trying to get God to come to me, instead I will enter into the place where He already is. Although such knowledge probably cannot pass through the tongue alone, I sometimes wish someone had told me this: when you avoid pain, above all else, you are avoiding God. This truth is not only for the affliction that finds me but also for the afflictions of others whom I could—with little effort—evade.

I believe this is a habit unique to those who follow the teachings of Christ. We are to seek out the gaping holes in the lives of others—initially out of sheer obedience to an invitation of presence within the wounds of others. But obedience gives way to passionate pursuit as God is encountered and discovered within the frame of pain.

Lost somewhere in the haze of Toddlerville with the rascals—Anders now a bald, big one-year-old, and Hazel is a talking two—I decided it would be a good time to abandon the job that actually paid me for my efforts in order to pursue leading the organization that we had started months after Eliot left us. I had reached a new state of desperation, longing to live out the lessons he had born in us. There was a nagging sense that dedicated effort for the children and families we had come to love—ones facing disability—was needed. Along the way I had become aware of the horrid plight faced by children with special needs in other countries. I stayed up nights dreaming up ways to change everything I was learning. God seemed steady in His pull, so I jumped and began working full time for 99 Balloons, reasoning that I had about six months to get others to see what was so clear to me.

In order to beg for support, I began inviting folks to home gatherings, telling them about the organization and our new direction. A local therapy clinic had been going to Ukraine and working with orphans with special needs—a country in which a diagnosis quite often means a life of neglect and stigma as many are hidden within government-run orphanages and institutions. I asked the therapists for one story of one child whom they were helping with their efforts, one story I could share in order to compel others to action.

They sent over pictures and information on a four-year-old girl named Lena. They chose her from all the other children due to the fact that she was closing in on a date when she would age-out of the orphanage and into an institution. It was a dark proposition they had witnessed in their visits and one that often ended with a life lost if the child were immobile. I shared the information they had gathered: Lena did not walk and did not talk. Photographs revealed a buzz-headed beauty with a smile mysteriously harboring some sort of misplaced joy.

I began asking those in attendance at the gatherings to pray for her and all she represented: discarded children, countries full of hidden individuals, rigid mind-sets arising from ideology, religion, and poverty. I pressed the team for more details on Lena as people asked me questions I was unable to answer. Her short haircut was the same given to all the other children in order to stave off lice. Lena's reality was hours upon hours in a crib. As I invited others to do so, Ginny and I began praying for Lena. Well, Ginny began praying for Lena.

People often ask how Eliot's life changed us. We always laugh—hard enough to make them feel foolish yet not long enough to offend—finishing the awkward routine by inquiring how much time they have. It's easy to see the good that our son's life brought to us—unspeakable gifts of clarity, faith, and love. However, the simple takes a turn toward the unfathomable when we're asked to see any good his leaving accomplished.

Every day of life since Eliot departed has allowed for a sort of complicated world in which there are two simultaneous movies playing out: one with him and one without him, because all we have in absence is imagination otherwise. The first universe is our real life, the moments we are living as they pass. The second is only make-believe and never requires conscious effort, a life playing out just as we would have scripted it—the life with Eliot in each scene, the one in which I am unable to take pictures at Hazel's birthday party because I am busy holding him, tending to whatever his current regiment would require. I don't think Ginny and I have ever had an actual conversation that acknowledged the existence of this alternate universe. However, we often take it for granted, sitting around after the unfolding of a day's events and discussing the variances had he been present.

So we always imagine that we could have done it better than God *did*—or *allowed*. Or insert whatever verb your beliefs will permit. Therein lies a pervasive scab that will not heal: the alternate universe is more beautiful than the one we occupy. When Eliot left, I closed the book on *optimal*, transitioning instead to *surviving, settling,* and *accepting.* The best was not to be.

Yet as of late I have had to acknowledge a mystery beyond my comprehension. For the first time I have seen with my own eyes that good has been brought forth from the whole—that the alternate universe cannot contain the one I am actually living.

February

I glance down our dossier checklist for adoption, looking for scribbled question marks indicating the areas in which we need help. The process and paperwork are daunting, but it is happening. We are pursuing a daughter halfway across the world with all our might. Somewhere in the midst of trying to awaken others, we found ourselves the target of awakening. *Why not?* If she is ours, would a lack of money or ill timing or any immeasurable distance hold us back?

Pausing for a prayer with no words, I acknowledge what I cannot understand. Eliot's life has led us here. And his hated absence is the only possible way we could be going where we are headed. I cannot script him in at this point, knowing that if he were here we would not be stepping in our current direction.

And I hate it. And I wish he were here more than anything—I always will. But I see beauty in the whole.

I see toil in the ashes.

I see mystery that a page cannot contain.

I see my son.

I see my daughter.

May

With eager longing, we await our dates to travel and bring her home, but I am not so naive as to think that the trip will be all rejoicing. There is mourning too—for a family who made the desperate decision to give her up, for a beautiful girl who has known abandonment and has only been dealt with in terms of her diagnosis rather than her humanity.

So our lives seem to return to the place that fairy tales seldom go—to where Eliot led us straightway. It is more complicated than our happy endings will allow. True life on this earth is a mess that comes only as a package deal, replete with a love so deep it will rip your flesh as it expands the sinews that hold us together. And it is good, and it is painful.

July

One week from today Ginny and I will weave together some hodgepodge of celebration and tears. The calendar will flip to July 20—Eliot's five-year birthday. This day will encompass a double portion of the oil that is our pain and the water that is our hope. For in addition to his birthday, it is also the precise deadline of when we are to receive a travel date from the State Department of Adoption in Ukraine to meet and bring home our daughter, Lena.

Chaos has been the precursor to our departure as we have busied ourselves with preparations. Our two-bedroom ranch home is currently a construction zone as teams of builders walk through our kitchen in a concerted effort to convert what was the garage into a bedroom for a girl we have never met.

We have been the recipient of varying reactions by others grappling to comprehend our excitement. We tend not to give information away unless pressed. From our vantage point, the short story, that we are awaiting travel dates to go and get our daughter, is sufficient, but often more questions come, and we prepare for any and all reactions to our forthcoming answers. Many have joined with us in this pursuit and excitement, and truth be told, we could never have reached this point without an entire community of support. For others, I feel that our family's decision somehow forces them to face realities they work hard to avoid. It is as if we, despite our best efforts otherwise, get to be witnesses to the awkward moment when their soul is divulged, and we're left feeling sheepish, though it is they who are naked. None of them are so bold as to express their thoughts to our faces, instead opting for thinly veiled opinions posed as questions: *What do we think this will do to our children? Have we thought this through?* And the one that is sure to send my head reeling with curses held captive: *What is her potential?*

I would like to espouse otherwise, but I get it. I really do. It becomes obvious to anyone watching this unfold that adopting a child with physical or mental impairments is in a different category altogether. Adoption is so strange. It allows a potential parent to weigh and question, to choose and decide—*What is all right for my child to have, and what is impermissible?* But when it's your flesh—your son or daughter—who's born with any ailment, you just start there and kill yourself trying to ensure him or her the best life.

Only one question was worth answering as we struggled with how to make the decision concerning whether we were to adopt her or not. *Is she our daughter?* We know that if she is, then we can do nothing but spend ourselves on loving her. Upon much prayer, thought, and discussion, we were bewildered to agree that, yes, she is.

This was the question that others should be asking of us: "Is she your daughter?" If so, then no distance or diagnosis will be sufficient to separate us. The anticipation of bringing her home and lining up the best care available in order for her to reach her potential is palatably exciting for us, but her potential is a conversation to come, having nothing do to with the decision of adoption.

In another twisted but well-meaning reaction, we are the noble couple—up high on the pedestal and worthy of a parade because we are adopting *her*. These are the blind ones, the ones who cannot see us for who we are—desperate, fearful, and seeking.

Open your eyes. If anyone is being saved, it is us.

Eighteen

AN UNFINISHED
REDEMPTION

It took us six weeks in Ukraine to meet
all the requirements before we were able
to walk out the orphanage gates with our
daughter. Those weeks apart from the rascals, now ages two and three, were nearly our
undoing—as Eliot left us a wee-bit fond of
time spent with our children. Nothing could
take us from our children except our child.
So we went.

I remember it as a cold and quiet drive. I had jumped in some European-model sedan to journey with our translator to Lena's hometown of Horlivka. My three companions spoke Russian as I sat sifting through thoughts and looking out the window as we approached the town where my soon-to-be daughter was born.

I saw her but for a second—a girl walking down a street within the town that Lena should be living in. And I lost my breath as it all played out in my head with a clarity it seemed I could reach out and touch.

But for disability, Lena would be living here, walking these streets. Instead, due to the effects of a lack of oxygen to her brain and resulting brain injury, she was dropped off at an orphanage where she spent countless hours neglected in a crib, her needs overwhelming the already overwhelmed staff.

But for losing my son, I would not be in this car. I would not be in Ukraine. I would not know how Lena dances when music plays. If Eliot were here, I would not be here.

The absolute worst thing in each of our lives was the very thing that brought us together. Without walking a road of pain and misery, our paths would never have crossed. But they did. Lena is my daughter. Though, if I were able, I would take away every ounce of the hurt she has known, it was the very path that allowed me to know her at all.

Along a potholed road in Horlivka, I see but a sliver of the good that is to come. And what I cannot fathom, I acknowledge.

ALL THINGS

The God who was with me in the pain and makes His home in the company of the hurting was a lesson quickly absorbed, beginning with the news that things with Eliot were not as we had hoped or imagined. But the rest has come only in time and remains in process, still coming fully into view.

And it is not about Eliot.

It is not about Lena.

And it most certainly is not about Ginny and me. It is about Him, present and at work in all and through all.

For His hands are dirty with the toil of making ashes beautiful. I must turn myself in here, although I fear that through my honesty you may see me for what I am.

I would take it all back if I were able—for five more minutes to hold him.

Were I to spin the worlds, the four arms of Ginny and me would be just enough for all four of them. For but a moment with my son, I would forfeit all the good that I have seen with my own eyes; I would return all the beauty that has been forged with pieces of my heart as the substance. More than once I have felt horrible for admitting what I always knew: the yield alone is not sufficient balm for the yearning of my soul.

So I find myself preempting the person who labors trying to put a bow on our story—awkwardly interrupting their valiant attempts at making sure that faith had set it all right, that we are okay with everything today, because apparently that is what their God does—He makes it all go away and sometimes even gives you a bigger house in the process.

But it is not all roses; it is not okay with me. I miss him every day.

Although I cannot deny God's presence and would readily admit being a witness of great work both in and through our loss, I could not with any conviction give onlookers the happy ending it seemed they so desperately sought. Upon my interruptions to let them know the way I felt, many exhibited horror typically reserved for child molesters, even while they insisted that time would be the magic wand that would make it all better—just as if it had never occurred.

It seemed to me that this objective created a lousy God, one who either takes away the very pain He led you to or mops up the mess caused by another. And while it seems that many just want me to move on, I do not sense that this is God's desire. For as He came near, dirtying His hands with the work of my ashes, He never diminished my pain, but He whispered of that to come.

Eternity is not a fantasyland warm fuzzy for me. As a believer, I maintain—with white-knuckled faith that defies my own logic—that heaven is a realm as real as the one I currently occupy. And I do not pretend to understand the dimensions, seemingly obscured by the One who knows. But I know enough; it is where the remaining portion of my yearning soul finds rest.

Jesus Christ has overthrown the power and effects of death.

I await the coming day when I join in the chorus questioning where death's sting has gone. The One who makes beauty from ashes in this world breathes life into ashes in the one to come. On this side we see in pieces the redemption that will one day come in full.

And I heard a loud voice from the throne saying, "Look! God's dwelling place is now among the people, and he will dwell with them. They will be his people, and God himself will be with them and be their God. He will wipe every tear from their eyes. There will be no more death or mourning or crying or pain, for the old order of things has passed away" (*Revelation 21:3-4*).

POSTSCRIPT

Lena has been home for eleven months now. She has crawled for the first time; she has spoken her first word—"Da-da-da-da" when I approach to pick her up. She took her first independent steps just weeks ago as her therapists hurriedly grabbed for their phones to video the moment—knowing we would not have believed it otherwise. It has been all sorts of hard and beautiful work, and each day's end is a triumph of sorts for Ginny and me in this season we occupy.

Ginny is not just a full-time mom but an *overtime* mom. She tries to document the daily affairs on her blog but typically opts to sleep in those all-too-rare available moments instead. She has recently begun a project she calls "Daily Hazel," snapping a photo of Hazel's self-chosen outfit each day, not wanting to let the goodness slip by within the craziness.

Hazel, now four, is a charmer. She follows instructions, helps out around the house, and busies herself with crafts of all sorts. But she has a tough side if you cross her and will let you know what she thinks. She is pretty-much the anti-Anders.

Anders is a three-year-old boy who can fathom no greater accomplishment than wrecking whatever Hazel just created. He thinks chase should be played during all hours that one is awake and loves to don a cape for nighttime. He is rough and tumble but heartbroken when corrected. They both interact with Lena in a way I could not have foreseen and never would have expected. My kids are teaching me how to love.

The work of 99 Balloons has greatly expanded, and we are in awe of the folks who have jumped in to change the story of disability. There are currently twelve—and counting—rEcess sites spread across numerous states as churches reach out to families within their communities who are experiencing disability. As we have shared the plight of children with disabilities abroad, others have responded by getting involved with projects for children with disabilities in Ecuador, Ukraine, Uganda, and Haiti. And it feels as though we are just beginning.

We miss him. We try to live out the lessons his sweet life brought us. And we watch it unfold in all its goodness; yet we set our gaze firmly on a day not yet here.

The story is not finished yet.

Matt's blog: www.theatypicallife.com
Ginny's blog: www.orbitofthemooneys.blogspot.com
Eliot's blog: www.mattandginny.blogspot.com
99 Balloons: www.99balloons.org

ENGAGING
individuals with
DISABILITY
LOCALLY & *GLOBALLY*

9 9 b a l l o o n s . o r g

building relationships
through serving families
affected by disability

*For information on bringing respite to your community,
visit 99balloons.org/local*